Charles Rennie
MACKINTOSH
Pocket Guide

John McKean

Colin Baxter Photography Limited, Grantown-on-Spey, Scotland

First published in Great Britain in 1998 by
Colin Baxter Photography Ltd, Grantown-on-Spey, Moray, Scotland
Revised 2000, 2001, 2004, 2007, 2010
Text Copyright © John McKean 2010
Photographs Copyright © Colin Baxter 1998
All rights reserved

www.colinbaxter.co.uk

The publishers would like to thank the following
for their kind permission to reproduce images in this book:

T&R Annan & Sons Ltd, Glasgow: 6
CRM Society: 30, 32, 33
Mrs Fisher: 4, 34, 35
Glasgow School of Art: 7, 9, 19, 21, 23, 25, 26, 29, 72
Hendersons the Jewellers: 50, 53, 54

Hunterian Art Gallery, University of Glasgow, Mackintosh Collection: 10, 13, 17, 60, 63, 64, 66, 67, 68, 69, 71
The National Trust for Scotland: 2, 38, 41, 42, 45, 46, 47, 48
Scotland Street School: 56, 59

Front Cover Photograph: Ladderback Chair, Main Bedroom, The Hill House
Back Cover Photograph: Porch Window, Windyhill
Page 2 Photograph: Detail, Bedroom Fireplace, The Hill House
Page 72 Photograph: Gentlemen's Cloakroom Door, Glasgow School of Art

A CIP catalogue record for this book is available from the British Library

ISBN 978-1-84107-356-9

Printed in China

Charles Rennie
MACKINTOSH
Pocket Guide

BIOGRAPHY

Charles Rennie Mackintosh (1868 - 1928) today offers a defining image of Glasgow. The work he completed in his native city, around a century ago, is known round the world. A major exhibition of his work toured the USA in 1996-7; his graphic imagery is mercilessly reproduced, his designed objects are copied and regurgitated, and now his interior spaces and even complete buildings are cloned.

The Charles Rennie Mackintosh Society is more than a powerfully active supporters' club. A fine interpretation of Mackintosh is a permanent display at The Lighthouse, which was formed in 1999 within the shell of Mackintosh's *Glasgow Herald* building in Mitchell Street. For the visitor to Mackintosh, the Society's headquarters at Queen's Cross, or The Lighthouse are obvious first ports of call.

Almost all Mackintosh's small architectural œuvre, as well as much of his furniture and decorative or illustrative work, is in and around Glasgow. But his brightly-lit fame these days also forces us all to judge for ourselves: to see what Mackintosh actually designed, through the layers which have been washed away from – or added to – his works.

By the 1920s there was a typical Mackintosh interior next door to his Willow Tea Rooms; it has vanished, and no-one today knows if it was an earlier, genuine Mackintosh or not. While today, in the Blue Room, upstairs in 'The New Willow Tea Rooms' in Buchanan Street (designed 50 years after his death), there is some very tasteful reconstruction, like the low 'Chinese' chairs; alongside which a tall-backed chair appears – but in a display case, as an exhibit. How confusing! Moreover many of Mackintosh's fitments were copied in his lifetime, can be again today, and anyway the originals are easily moved: the cover of one book on the Glasgow School of Art is an illustration of the stair light

◄ Throwing light in a Mackintosh interior. The purity, simplicity and subtle charm of the little drop pendant over the square porch window at Windyhill (1900), with its 10 by 10 leaded squares.

from a Mackintosh house which happens now to be in the Art School collection.

But Mackintosh was not the lone martyr whose life deserves memorialising with all the accoutrements, the sale of relics and the tawdry memorabilia of a local saint. He was a tirelessly inventive designer and, more importantly, a great

architect. Much of his work was shared with his lifelong and devoted partner Margaret Macdonald, an artist and very talented designer in her own right. They, along with another couple, Margaret's sister Frances and Herbert McNair, were for a very brief time, exactly a century ago, known as 'The Four'. This quartet was deeply embedded in a much wider group of innovative and lively designers and artists of the Glasgow Style. This wider style was closely influenced by nationalist and Celtic

Mackintosh aged 25, photographed by Annan in 1893 not as the assistant architect but as the interior artist.

revivalist ideas in Scotland, by the Arts & Crafts and the Aesthetic Movements in England, and not least by the great centres of European contemporary design of the moment, most obviously fin-de-siècle Vienna.

The extraordinary, sudden and brief flowering of art nouveau across Europe and even the USA around 1900, gave Mackintosh a sudden fame as decorator of the artistic interior. Even before the bright flame of that fashion went, as quickly as it came, Mackintosh had outgrown it, to become one of the few great original architects of the time.

In the late 1880s, the young Mackintosh had entered a double world – the practical, masculine and dour world of construction, and the bright, romantic and feminine world of art. An apprentice architect by day, his evenings and weekends were spent with friends wrapped in symbolic and allegorical image making. They called themselves 'The Immortals', and within this group were formed The Four. The few formative years of their intense collaboration in the mid 1890s were of great importance. Mackintosh and Margaret married in 1900 and the work became inextricable; he would sign drawings 'CRM – MMM'. (The use of one set of initials in this text always recalls the unspoken other half of this double signature.)

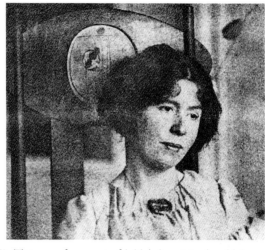

Macdonald, in an 1899 CRM chair, probably photographed before their marriage in 1900.

In 1893, having assisted and detailed various buildings and extensions in the office of Honeyman & Keppie, CRM designed the first new building we recognise as his: the *Glasgow Herald* warehouse (now The Lighthouse). This, and the Martyrs' School which followed in 1895 (p57), both show glimpses of unusual talent, but neither is architecturally remarkable. At the same time, he began designing furniture, if not yet with an individuality we recognise as his own.

In 1896, Honeyman & Keppie was invited to compete for Glasgow's new Art School. One of their entries, clearly designed by 28-year-old Mackintosh, won (p18). The governors only had money for half, which was built over three years and opened at the end of 1899. Later, they decided to complete the project, and Mackintosh, now fully in control, completely revised a new west end. Finished exactly a decade later, this masterpiece was virtually both his first and his last building. CRM's architectural work is almost all that of a man in his thirties.

As the School of Art was rising, with John Keppie running the job on site (and even claiming the design as his), CRM continued to produce furniture and illustration on his own. In 1896, the commission to stencil decoration for a tea room in Buchanan Street started CRM's long association with his most faithful patron, Kate Cranston. He designed her no new buildings; simply a wonderful succession of tea room interiors, furniture, decoration, cutlery and even waitresses' costumes, in existing city-centre blocks. He also refitted and furnished her own Glasgow house. Most of all this invention is now lost, and none – apart from the first floor of one tea room – remains in place today.

In 1897, while in the daytime as architect designing his only church (p31), CRM's other life as Artist was first noticed; *The Studio* illustrated a mural and some furniture. Then, alongside the small Ruchill church hall (p33), came much furniture for Miss Cranston's tea room at 114 Argyle Street. His range of seating and light-fittings here includes the famous dark oak chairs, with their tall back legs and two vertical flats ending in an oval disc above the seater's head through which a bird flies (p63).

In the last days of the century, the Art School, an odd half-building, was opened, filled and fitted with CRM's latest furniture and interior ideas including the masterly Director's suite. He now designed the printing office for another local paper, *The Daily Record* which, like the earlier *Glasgow Herald* building, required only a conventional block and got an unconventional skin. At the same time, in the utterly contrasting location

▶ *The rose was the central symbol of the Glasgow Style around 1900, taken to its most abstract and graphic, as well as its widest range of representation, by CRM-MMM. From their Rose Boudoir in Turin in 1902, it is echoed in MMM's gesso panels, in inlaid furniture, metalwork at the School of Art, lightfittings and leaded glass, stencilling on chair upholstery and around interior walls. This example is on a bookcase for Windyhill (1901) now in the Glasgow School of Art.*

of an open suburban hillside, Mackintosh designed his first large detached house. In Kilmacolm, 14 miles (22.5 km) south-west of Glasgow, Windyhill (p35) was also his first building whose exterior image seemed entirely based on a harled, unornamented Scottish vernacular. This important house has turned its back successfully to the public since it was built, and it holds its privacy to this day. (It is almost always illustrated by a photograph of the back, and is not accessible to the public.)

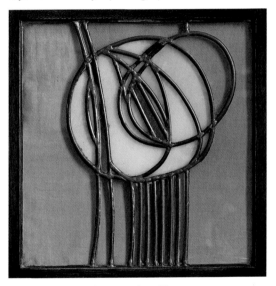

When they married in 1900, MMM and CRM fitted out their own first-floor apartment at Blythswood Square (p61) and then, in Ingram Street, created their first large-scale tea room interior, the Ladies' Luncheon Room. Late that year, The Four were invited by Josef Hoffmann, the Viennese architect, and his colleagues J M Olbrich and Gustav Klimt, to take part in a Vienna Secession exhibition. CRM later called it the trip of his lifetime. The Mackintoshes designed their own room, and filled it with both the atmosphere of their new flat and some real pieces of their home furniture. The exhibition was praised and became influential among designers; CRM furniture was fitted into a Hoffmann-designed house.

While there, the Mackintoshes heard about and entered a German publisher's competition for 'a house for an art lover.' Although their entry could not be considered a winner because it was incomplete, when the sponsor published portfolios of the three best projects, one was the Mackintosh. Thus it was possible that, nearly a century later, this dream house is somewhat realised in Bellahouston Park (p36). Meanwhile, back in the real world, Mackintosh got down to detail design at Windyhill, whose shell was nearly built – forming its interior spaces, fitments and

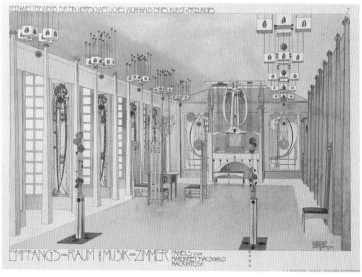

fittings – and he entered the competition for a vast Liverpool Cathedral in which he was not placed.

In 1902, they exhibited again in Europe (in Turin), and a German magazine published the most serious account of the Mackintoshes' work that would appear in their lifetimes. This publication also included the design for an Artist's Cottage in the country – one of a couple of abstract, client-free projects of great simple charm. (These drawings have also recently been used as the basis of a reconstruction, near Inverness.) Francis Newbery, head of the Glasgow School of Art, organised the 'Scottish section' in Turin; CRM was architect and, with MMM, created the exquisite room setting 'The Rose Boudoir'. Invitations to exhibit in Dresden, Moscow and Berlin (if not in Britain) soon followed. In Vienna, the Mackintoshes used their collaborative skills to produce their most complete artistic interior – a music room for Fritz Wärndorfer, a wealthy Secessionist supporter. Now CRM's domestic masterpiece The Hill House was being designed (p39) and the finest tea rooms, The Willow (p52), begun.

In mid-1903, while The Willow was being fitted out, CRM landed the job of a large new Glasgow board school in Scotland Street (p58). Then, while that school was going up, he created the interiors of The Hill House and those for the main rooms of Miss Cranston's old southside mansion, Hous'hill. Here he had a free hand with the interiors, creating half a dozen complete room settings, and even more furniture than for The Hill House. (The interiors for Wärndorfer were dispersed or destroyed by 1916; at Hous'hill it was another 15 years before the furniture was dispersed (mostly lost) and the house and its fitments then demolished by its owners, Glasgow Corporation, after a fire. All we have of either are one or two endlessly reproduced photographs.)

It is difficult in a short tale to avoid the impression that there was no local context within which the Mackintoshes lived and worked. There were obviously artistic and architectural allegiances as well as enmities. A visit to the Art Galleries, being built at the same time as the Art School, gives a good turn-of-the-century context. This building itself is both overwhelming and vulgar. An 1892 competition-winner, by English academic architects Simpson & Allen, it beat 24-year-old CRM's eclectic and highly decorated juvenile extravaganza, as well as Honeyman's mediocre neo-Greek and Keppie's conventional and clumsy Beaux-Arts entries.

Six years later, for the International Exhibition of 1901 to be sited alongside the new Art Galleries,

◄ Music and reception room in the House for an Art Lover. As CRM's ceilings usually do, this one vanishes; here the avenue of tapering posts just touches the vault with tiny green leaves. Between the bay windows and this line of posts, he drops a rail which hides the window-heads, and binds this long space within its aesthetic grove.

▶ *Mackintosh drew flowers all his life, but was particularly prolific during his stay in Walberswick, Suffolk, from 1914 to 1915. It was there that he made this exquisite study of* Fritillaria. *The plant's chequered petals are actually precisely observed, though they might seem (as nature following art) to be created as a CRM stylisation.*

a more mature and independent CRM competed for the buildings. While the winners were again all elaborately decorated wedding cakes, in keeping with the Art Galleries, CRM had now abandoned all that baggage. His beautiful drawings rely on subtle curves and simple forms. His 'alternative concert hall' proposal, with its coolly shaped shallow dome to seat 4221, shows the contrast best.

Relics from 1901 are still in the collection of Glasgow Museums – room settings by E A Taylor, John Ednie, George Logan and George Walton, fine Glasgow Boys paintings, a beautiful Talwin Morris mirror which had been at the Turin 1902 exhibition, and there are CRM candlesticks and cutlery, alongside as much as they can show of his Ingram Street tea room furniture.

By 1904 however, art nouveau was as past as the mysterious, grotesquely attenuated figures in the 'spook school' paintings of The Four. The changing architectural context is shown in the work of James Salmon, which develops astonishingly from 'The Hatrack' (1899-1902), Glasgow's finest art nouveau block in Bath Street, to Lion Chambers (1904-7), a stern reinforced-concrete block in Hope Street. Salmon and his good friend Mackintosh (or 'wee Troutie' and 'Toshie' as they were known) used to be annoyed (I quote Salmon) 'that nobody else is proud enough of Glasgow to be ashamed of it.' Salmon's relationship with a more classical and less inventive partner, remarkably similar to CRM's experience, was to end in 1913.

In the first decade of the century, CRM was at the peak of his career. He moved up in the world with MMM from their rented flat to purchase a terrace house in the West End, in a fashionable middle-class suburb by the university. This building, offering the closest contact with their domestic intimacy, is today the ideal choice for those who have only time for one Mackintosh visit (p61).

Early in 1907, Mackintosh's practice (he was now Keppie's partner) was commissioned to complete the School of Art and, exactly a decade after the first phase, it was opened in December 1909. We might expect to see the architect, now aged 41, at the height of his powers, about to produce the work of his maturity. Extraordinarily, apart from a few tea rooms and one little domestic fit-out, CRM had little work again.

By 1910 Mackintosh was seen as old-fashioned. There was no new work; he became depressed and drank heavily. His strongest supporter, Fra Newbery, also became depressive and ground down by running the Art School where the less talented Keppie, as governor and then chairman, was increasingly powerful, and the new head of architecture was conspicuously pro Franco-American and anti any Austro-Germanic influence. J J Burnet, whose role on the Art School building committee was to keep tight rein on CRM's creativity, was now building his classically ordered galleries for the British Museum in London. This was seen as the future.

In 1913, CRM failed to complete a scheme for a competition which was won by the banal entry of a junior in their office, A Graham Henderson. Henderson was soon made a partner on the strength of it, Mackintosh by that time had agreed that his partnership should end. (Henderson later became CRM's sharpest critic and the source of nasty stories about his unprofessionalism.)

By now Mackintosh was suffering from extreme depression and severe pneumonia. Giving up hope of independent architectural practice in Glasgow, in 1914 the Mackintoshes retreated to the New-

berys' holiday village in Suffolk, perhaps aiming to continue to Vienna. But once there, and with the European War breaking out, they stayed a year. In a complete break from architecture, CRM became absorbed in the most elegant and delicate botanical sketches and watercolours (over forty survive). Then, amidst the xenophobic hysteria drummed up to support the war, traumatically, CRM was picked up as a spy. Ordered out of East Anglia, the Mackintoshes escaped to the more congenial bohemian world of Chelsea, the artists' corner of London, staying for eight years.

In 1916, W J Bassett-Lowke, industrialist, model-maker and modernist, searched out CRM to convert his pokey terrace house in Northampton. Mackintosh added a shallow bay at the back; a cool, white rectangular box, facing the river to the south, which gave a touch of spaciousness to the bottom floors, framed a balcony to the main bedroom and gave a terrace to the guest room on top. But what impresses in the interior of 78 Derngate, Northampton, which has now been restored, is the use of bold, deep colour and jagged forms amidst a shiny dark. The powerful originality of both hall and guest bedroom is also clear in their reconstructions – the hall and stair screen for the 1996 exhibition; the bedroom in the gallery above the Mackintosh House in the Hunterian (p71).

In 1917 CRM also did one final tea room for Miss Cranston: a basement room, dug out under the Willow. CRM and MMM both designed textiles for various manufacturers (a few hundred designs survive, mostly in the Hunterian), in bright, geometric patterns, brilliant and subtle colours. The 1919 guest room at Derngate (p71) was his last built work.

In their corner of Chelsea, artist friends 'commissioned' studios, but although CRM got as far as mugging-up the LCC bye-laws, obtaining quotations for building in reinforced concrete, and submitting elevations to the ground landlord (who demanded 'more architectural qualities'), nothing came of them. The elevation to Glebe Place of three studios, a composite drawing of projects on adjoining sites designed over a year or more from early 1920, gives a hint of what a remarkable group London (and the subsequent development of British architecture before the Second World War) lost. It could have broken CRM through to a new career. But there never seems to have been the will to pursue them.

In 1920, Bassett-Lowke covered CRM's extraordinary dark hall and stair in light grey; he then asked Mackintosh to design another decorative scheme, and got a frieze in jazzy triangles and lozenges, but much lighter than before. In 1925 the frieze was used again in the Bassett-Lowkes' new, larger house, designed – because they could not track Mackintosh down – by the famous German designer, Peter Behrens.

For, the Mackintoshes had left Britain; heading for the Mediterranean, where, for four years, they lived in cheap hotels, finally stopping in Port-

◀ *Mackintosh's 1916 remodelling of the door at 78 Derngate, Northampton. This original door is too fragile to reinstate at the restored house. Instead, a replica, painted in the original black, has been installed. Bassett-Lowke had been recommended CRM. This conversion was to be Mackintosh's last architectural commission. By the mid-1920s, when Bassett-Lowke searched for the architect again, for a new house, CRM could not be found, having abandoned both architecture and Britain.*

Vendres, near the Franco-Spanish border. Here, having abandoned architecture for a second and now final time, CRM concentrated on developing his watercolours towards a new vision (41 landscapes survive). Finally, illness forced Margaret back to England, soon followed by Mackintosh whose painful mouth was diagnosed as cancer. He died in December 1928, aged sixty. Margaret, never again settled or well, outlived him by just five years. On her death, all their things were valued: his drawings and everything from the studio, all their furniture including several CRM chairs and all the French paintings. The total valuation was under £90.

What was Mackintosh's position in the world of architecture? Just into the twentieth century, when in his early thirties, CRM was hailed by the Viennese Secessionists as 'our leader… who showed us the way;' and, for a German critic, in 'the list of truly original artists, the creative minds of the modern movement, the name of Charles Mackintosh would certainly be included even among the few that one can count on the fingers of a single hand.' Later, in 1913, a gathering of European architects and designers in Poland toasted: 'to our mentor Mackintosh, the greatest since the gothic.' Yet that was just when he was abandoning architectural practice, leaving Glasgow to spend the remaining years unpublished and in private obscurity. (No image of the Glasgow School of Art was published before 1924; no plan till 1950.)

For whatever reasons the Mackintosh career was not that of a successful architect. CRM-MMM worked privately and together, with little attributed to MMM alone after their marriage. Though extraordinarily talented, CRM was assistant and then partner in an ordinary architectural practice.

It is astonishing to remember, when we look back to the first decade of the century – seeing the wealth of decorative work, the great range of objects (over sixty chair designs are documented), the drawings and paintings, the remarkable interiors

► *Mackintosh abandoned architectural practice in 1921, in his early fifties. Isolated in a Mediterranean village, in the few years he had left, CRM became a landscape watercolourist of extraordinary quality. His vision is calm and unpeopled. In* Rue du Soleil *(1926), which is in the collection of the Hunterian Art Gallery, the water is almost solid geometry; pattern and colour dominate an almost abstract composition.*

carved out within existing shells, and the few masterly buildings – that this man was born at the same time as Frank Lloyd Wright and only a decade before Le Corbusier, who were both building major works in the late 1950s, two generations after CRM's career had virtually ended.

Nikolaus Pevsner, the great mid twentieth cen-

tury architectural historian, researched for an essay just after Mackintosh's death. When published (much later) in English, it ended: 'He was a genius. He had a spatial imagination as fertile and complex as those of Frank Lloyd Wright and Le Corbusier... I never knew Mackintosh, but at the same time I have never met anyone – and I have approached many of his friends and contemporaries – who did not speak of him with a light in their eyes.'

GLASGOW SCHOOL OF ART

Francis Newbery, who became head while CRM was an evening student in architecture (and indeed the first Scottish student to win a Gold Medal for architecture) brought to the Glasgow School of Art an inspirational and international leadership. He wanted a new building; in 1894 his governors began to find funds and a site; by 1896 a dozen local architectural practices were invited to compete for its design. Whatever was his role in the choice of winner, Newbery and his wife Jessie became and remained Mackintosh's firm friends for life.

▶ 'Portals must have guardians', CRM read in Lethaby, the contemporary English architectural writer whose work he quoted. Here they are: the symbolic women flanking a stylised rosebush, holding the clue to the art-world of The Four. Directly over the entrance to the School of Art, as the building's literal keystone, this (1897-8) is the only ornamented stonework on the building.

The winning scheme was designed in the second half of 1896, just two years after CRM had completed his part-time education there. Its layout, responding directly to the utilitarian brief and very tight finances, is very straightforward: a central entrance on the main lower floor climbs straight into the heart of the building. There, directly ahead, the top-lit stair leads up to the 'museum', the school's hub, next to the director's office above the entrance. Studios range to right and left on the two main floors, on the north side of long corridors; two lecture rooms, as required by the brief, are at opposite far ends, north-east corner on ground floor (which later became a studio) and south-west corner on the floor below. The land sloped steeply to the south allowing considerably more accommodation below the entrance level, although no windows were allowed on the enclosed site boundary which might be built up to by southern neighbours. The simple E-shape plan has top-lit basement studios filling the gaps in the E to the south.

At first the governors could only afford to build half; starting with the east end and central core. A decade later, when they were able to complete it, Mackintosh redesigned the west end and added a top layer of studios the length of the building, set back from the facade. The great north front, which in 1985 the US architect Robert Venturi called 'one of the greatest achievements of all time, comparable in scale and majesty to Michelangelo', was not changed.

In narrow Renfrew Street, with the rhythm of three huge studio windows one side and four the other, and the picturesque intricate composition of the central masonry element, visitors seldom realise that the entrance is precisely in the centre. The symmetrical railing and street wall add a syncopated rhythm. Subtle massing of the central form is framed by the geometry of the austere studio windows on either side, each under the great brim of their cap. It is

more than two art factories which hem in a lovable old castle. In the centre is the complex (and ambiguous) hub on top of which sits the director. Spread alongside are the mono-dimensional, focused (and clear) activities of the studios.

Look at the dynamic balance of the central composition: the oriel window to the left of the door, cut by the balcony which also separates the entrance from its formal cap, the great arch headed window. Further up, the tower stair, far taller than necessity would dictate, rises to the director's private (recessed, shady) studio. To the sides, the studio rhythm is detailed with rolled masonry edges to the great windows hitting their sharply cut, recessed but expressed steel lintels. (Note the one tiny window between two great studios; it lights a model's changing space.) The rest of the metalwork we can see here humanises surfaces, articulates silhouette and edges, and enriches with metaphor: the delicate iron brackets with their individual flowery open knots in front of the plain window framing; the finials atop the towers; the individual symbolic discs on the street edge rising from their clumps of wrought-iron tulips. Perhaps it is important we are not told all their meanings.

▶ *The astonishing vertical sweep of the great library windows at the south-west corner of the School of Art (1907-8), outlined in crisply detailed and geometrically sharp masonry frames. To the right, on the south flank, the window forms are sunk into the harled surface.*

Before entering, look at the building flanks. The east wall in Dalhousie Street remains from the 1890s, an asymmetrical composition with obviously picturesque baronial touches. The right half, being the side wall of the studios, naturally, is blank (windows beside the basement door are later changes). On the left, the scale changes dramatically as it runs steeply down hill, here with its own symmetry of bow windows (for the board room) over the heavy rounded pediment of the staff room double window.

Walking to the other side, there is no clue on the great north front that, beyond the front steps, this half face is a decade newer; nor can the additional floor of studios, set back from the edge, be seen from the pavement. Then we turn the corner into Scott Street.

Now the decade's development seems more like a century removed from the eastern end. The great blank, uncoursed wall of dressed rubble with its one romantic, tiny window, flanking the studios, remembers its ancient cousin, the opposite bookend in Dalhousie Street. But now, layered onto this, is new masonry work formed with the sharp skill CRM had recently honed at Scotland Street School, here used with fearless incisiveness. Six identically cut ground-floor bays march across this wall; and from the southern three, oriels soar up, 62 ft (19 m) to their triangular gable. All this is articulated in carefully coursed ashlar, held in an utterly precise geometry of solid articulated bays of stratified glass, masked with the small square net of bronze framing (which replaced the original iron in 1947) and masonry courses. In the centre are the three great library windows, with half-cylinders of masonry flanking them, intended for

never-executed sculptures. Down the hill, looking round the corner to the south, the west block is built up to the property line over which no projections were allowed. So while the west is modelled beyond the wall-plane, on the south it is all within the plane. Here the articulated bays repeat, the symmetrical composition responding to that round the corner, but now sunk as if disappearing into the harled surface's quicksand.

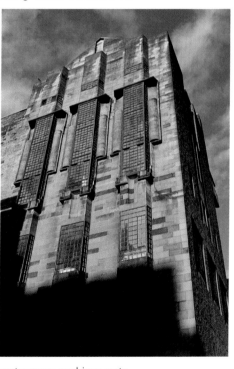

Before leaving the west end, as we climb back past the sub-basement screen and iron gateway, look at the strange basement level door on Scott Street; so staggered and layered, with its Mannerist reversals as always in CRM's formal playing, like the shadowy keystone. If we did not know, we might wonder when it was built; and, more interesting than calling it 'proto Deco' and so on, wonder why it was built? What did CRM mean by all this layering of planes and lines? It certainly worried the governors' sense of financial economy when, on a site visit with only the basement built, they looked uncomprehendingly at its complexity!

Robert Venturi's comparison with Michelangelo is not hyperbole. In his 1968 book *Complexity and Contradiction in Architecture*, Venturi was the first author after the era of Modernism to deal with the great Mannerist architects, from Michelangelo to Hawksmoor to Lutyens. Mackintosh, in forming the skin of this west block, now had a fluent command of his language; in his reversals of the rules, hinted at in earlier projects, in the final phase of the School of Art he is playing in this company.

To enter, we must climb back to Renfrew Street. Up the tightening steps enclosed by curving walls and under the great knot – the symbolic women flanking a stylised rose bush as the building's literal key stone – which is the building's only ornamented stonework. Directly beneath stands one dead central timber column. At first the porch was open (which makes sense of the janitor's enquiry hatch on the left). When doors had to be added, right at the top of the steps, (they not only say 'art' and 'school' in CRM's inimitable finger-print, but also 'in' and 'out', to avoid awful accidents), he hung onto the column's importance by hanging the doors from it, rather than from the sides as we might expect. Entering these narrow-est of actual doors, what an astonishing change of scale is forced by this compression! (Note the squares of glass of the hatch to the left and three bright blue, welcoming glass hearts in the inner door frames ahead.) Then the odd different sym-metry of the entrance hall is suddenly revealed, tightly held among solid, squat columns under a crypt's low vault. The pillars to the left become revealed as central in a double space, widened into a pausing place, and now opening into the shop. Today, guided tours start here and my description follows the usual route.

Straight ahead, the stairs rise to the light of the school's central exhibition space. Here, in this steel and concrete building, is a timber cage of overlap-

▶ *Approaching the door to the Headmaster's office (or director, as we say today), showing how CRM (in 1898-9) touches the door, 'plain building' (as was required by his client body) with details of great charm at the points to which our eyes and bodies come close. (Every door at the School of Art is worth noticing; see also p72.)*

ping square balustrading and tall newels, some coming right up from the basement floor, others continuing up to the roof trusses flanking the stairwell. As we rise, and our eyes look further up, we see it is covered with almost barn-like wooden trusses softened by little hearts, inspired by Voysey, cut into their posts. Those round the stair are carried on the timber columns; however, those to the sides have column caps simply floating in the

space. Thus Mackintosh's mannerist games continue. (Note on the stair, by the way, Glasgow's coat of arms, the remarkable iron rod abstraction of a tree which supports rather more literal bell, bird and fish.)

To the north, the director has a dark threshold across which, unfortunately, you probably will not be invited into his private sanctum today. If you manage to penetrate for a moment, it is well worth it. The door opens into another world: bright yet enclosed. In here the cornice both holds the pure cube of the room, tying in the lovely concealed stair to his private studio above, plus storage and a WC, and breaks it, flowing gently into the deep window bay, its vault seeming scooped out of the thickness of the wall, like a castle window's deep embrasure.

Moving along the corridor to the east, look up at the shapes made by the bellying cuts of the light-wells in the black-framed ceiling under the lean-to roof-lights beyond. If possible (and other than at diploma show time it may not be), look in to the left, at one of the great, working studios; direct, industrially formed machines for capturing and diffusing light. (These nearly 33 ft (10 m) tall spaces, with 8 ft (2.5 m) wide hidden, flat roof-lights, have from the start had hot air central heating.) The lower 10 ft (3 m) of the dividing cross-walls between these studios used to be removable: what an astonishing layered, horizontal space that must have been with them stacked away.

There was originally only the central stair, and when escape stairs were required at either wing, one enclosed the board room's west-facing bay windows. It is said the board refused to use this room; and certainly before 1909, when the stair wrapped it, this was a design studio. In 1947 it became 'The Mackintosh Room'. This is not a Mackintosh setting; but in here is a variety of CRM furniture, chairs from the range of tea rooms and, among other artifacts, one of MMM's finest gesso panels, *The Heart of the Rose*. Note the light fittings (particularly the magnificent central one) which all came from Windyhill. Also from that house came perhaps the most impressive object: the long, dark bookcase. Hanging on the wall alongside is an earlier drawing for a toy-chest (note the side shelves below for 'hammers tools etc' and the end doors above to hide books). Being too massive for the Davidsons' playroom, it was redesigned with considerably more elegance (for which the final drawing was given to the Art School by Tom Howarth). It is a wonderful, if scarcely domestic, object; its four leaded rose

▶ *The tiniest Mackintosh detail is handled with a charm and appropriateness; neither overdone nor thrown away. The slightly projecting, identical cement squares on every half-landing of the east and west stairs each contain a different number of differently coloured 3 in square (70 mm) glazed tiles.*

panels (see p9) like the brilliant designs on an out-stretched black silk kimono.

The stair, which just misses those bay windows, giving us a tiny theatrical frisson of outside / inside ambiguity, rises to the top studios. On the barest, almost medieval walls with their grey polished plaster, little squares of square coloured tiles attract the eye and fingers at each half-landing; every one is different. It is again the mix of sturdiness and delicacy, which CRM handles with unrivalled sureness – just like the tiny eyes of coloured leaded glass in the black doors and their rough corridors. And then at the top, reminding us that this stair was designed after those at Scotland Street (p58), we reach the portcullis, where a cage of metal flats under a circle veils the junction of masonry with timber roof. A dark dungeon in the air, before we move along and out to the dramatic opposite extreme: the fragile, perilous passageway in the sky.

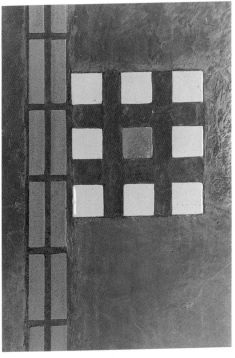

To link east and west when this additional top floor was added, Mackintosh didn't break into the existing central tower (the director's studio). Instead he cantilevered a walkway (always known as the 'hen-run') off its south wall, a light timber net enclosed only in glass.

This fragile passage leads to a vaulted loggia, whose bays offer the best view in Glasgow,

beyond Alexander Thomson's St Vincent Street Church and away to the south. There is no better place, in any building in Britain, for students to sit quietly working or to loiter – were it not the threshold to the professors' private studios! Before descending, stick your nose if at all possible into the studio straight ahead at the end of the loggia (room 58). This is the Composition Room above the library; the one studio with a south window, which also has, hanging off its south-east corner, the extraordinary little conservatory you saw from the loggia, for the precision plant studies at which CRM himself so excelled. To look at the tiniest of plants in the brightest light, high in the sky, was a touch of pure romance. (This conservatory appears on the very first, otherwise exceedingly plain south elevation, the competition drawing of 1896.) Note this studio's freestanding columns (steel) and beams (timber) with their spare Japanese austerity, the geometry of the three low cuts in the gable and see how the bays, so prominent up to the cornice on the outside, become solid masonry inside.

Down half a storey, the former book store above the library now shows off a Mackintosh furniture collection. It was not designed as a pleasant public space. But, while admiring its contents, enjoy the room's qualities too: look out of the windows, and especially down into the library oriels. Note also the ingenious structure: the floor (which is the library ceiling) is suspended from the low steel beams by eight pairs of twisted straps.

The west stair continues down to the library, and through its leaded glass doors, into the sacred grove of knowledge. The forest clearing, its trees silhouetted against the brightness beyond; the grouped lamps hanging on chains from darkness, with their jangling detail, folded structures of black and silver, hole-punched, metal flats around naked light bulbs, abstract, exotic birds with their touches of blue and pink glass, their dazzle veiling the dark canopy above. Never can the arrival at this moment

◀ *Spatially, the library (1909) is Mackintosh's tour-de-force. Complex, intricate and yet intimate, it is extraordinarily difficult to contain in a photograph. Carrying the narrow gallery across the tall windows, which fly up past yet another storey, was controversial from the start. In January 1909 the client committee objected that it would jeopardise the interior light. However, at a committee meeting which its architect members (led by J J Burnet) were unable to attend, CRM cheekily argued that it would be too expensive at this late stage in the process to change the design by removing it. Mackintosh won his balcony.*

27

of electricity in architecture have been better celebrated than in these fittings from 1909.

The central clearing is formed by eight wide trees, whose thick lower trunks are made up of three pieces; the outer two branch back to support the gallery, while the central trunk continues up, joining other thinner verticals from the gallery, to the forest canopy of crisscrossed branches. Underneath such metaphors, just as under the decorated, scalloped almost frilled surfaces, the interior spatial geometry is precisely controlled and clearly articulated. And the structure all ties together; the columns standing on great steel joists in the floor just touch the ceiling, each being tied up to the twisted hangers from the higher steels we saw in the room above.

If you know this space from photographs, its intimate scale can be a shock. (It is only 36 ft (11 m) square.) Note the central table, with five perforated and carved uprights at each end; the screen and periodical rack with its tiny glass inserts at the top was wrapped round it some years later by CRM. Similar decoration appears on the laths of the gallery front, where you will see that no two combinations of holes are identical.

On three sides the gallery sits on cranked beams, back from the supporting columns; but CRM's boldest move was to carry it across the windows. Unfortunately, with its narrow stair and limited space above, this area cannot be accessible to visitors. But move under it.

The spaces formed between the worlds of inside and out are always among the most telling in CRM's work, but this transitional place is exceptional. You cannot walk into it, but poke your head in and look up; sense the elements and enclosure and the gallery reverse bays which create extraordinary hexagonal columns of space rising above you.

We finally must mention the board room, though it is not usually open to the public. Here

▶ *Mackintosh designed many clock faces, each appropriate to its purpose (there are very different ones on p38 and p68; also in The School of Art, in the director's room, is a beautiful standing clock from the Willow Tea Rooms). This face is one of a group of similar but not all identical electric wall clocks, mounted in public places round the school and controlled from a master.*

in 1906, the board who so disliked their original tall white space, found a new, stuffy, classical home, carved out of a ground floor studio. Dark and enclosed, it is a most unusual room. (Look up at the ceiling, a heavy mesh of layers of structure, and at the three extraordinary clusters of hammered copper light fittings in delicate wrought iron, under it.) Certainly there never have been Ionic capitals like the eight, each different, here.

Was this space Mackintosh's ironic comment on the new classical orthodoxy of Edwardian academic architecture by the time the building was finished? Much of the unhappiness in the story of CRM and the School of Art can be read from Newbery's group portrait of governors which hangs in this room: the architect was added on an additional strip of canvas at the left after the portrait had been approved. His expression is honestly captured.

This building began as Mackintosh's masterpiece, in the old sense of the piece which ends an apprenticeship, honours mastery of the skill, and heralds a mature career. It gained him his partnership, after all. And it ends as his masterpiece, in the modern sense, because it developed after the seven-year gap of CRM's confident career, into something quite different. It is also his masterpiece, as we so easily see in retrospect, because there simply weren't any others which followed.

CHURCHES

Mackintosh's one church is St Matthew's Free Church, at Queen's Cross, north-west of central Glasgow. Having become redundant, it was taken over by the Charles Rennie Mackintosh Society whose headquarters it has been since 1977. Early in 1897 he designed this building at the junction of two main roads, Garscube and Maryhill, on Glasgow's northern edge. Its picturesque image in a simple, gothic revival form is dominated by the tapering and cut off corner tower, directly based on a real medieval one which had been sketched by Mackintosh in Somerset a year or two earlier. The turret (precisely copied from the English church, and an extravagant flourish here to house a simple gallery stair) grows from its side, and rises to a lookout.

On the main road, there are four quite different groups of bays: a high pair, a low pair and the end ones each with a door. Below a tracery window in the corner tower is the main entrance; in the porch tower at the eastern end – and under a peculiar and beautifully carved column which splits the window overhead – is the minor entrance. Today both are closed. To get in, you must walk round the corner into Springbank Street, passing below the large art-nouveau-gothic window, to the vestry door where the bell is answered by the CRM Society during opening hours.

The masonry forms and details are full of imaginative play, but once inside we see that it is more than just decorative surface. The two entrances, we now realise, do not come directly into the church but enter vestibules from which, turning right or left, we either go up to a gallery or enter the side of this large, barn-like preaching hall, in an ambiguous aisle underneath its side gallery.

If its simplicity pleased the Free Church, its unexpected asymmetry added a dynamism to that

◀ *Looking from the back gallery across Queen's Cross Church (1897), the slight asymmetries are made clear in this axial view: the west window does not quite align with the lamp over the chancel entrance, the communion table and the not-quite-central aisle. The building's major asymmetry, however, just out of shot to the left, is the side gallery, which juts into the nave from its own space beyond the barrel vault.*

essentially static space. The side gallery beyond the main roof, under its own two gabled bays and bearing little obvious relation to the church's interior space, is said to derive from a Japanese inn which Mackintosh knew from a book.

The details in the church interior, which is now restored to good condition, are full of invention. From the beautifully (and strangely) carved pulpit, past the lamp over the centre of the chancel

Detail of the Queen's Cross Church pulpit carving; with abstracted bird and botanical imagery closely relating to CRM's symbolic painting of the mid 1890s.

entrance, our eyes wander upwards and unexpectedly meet the rivets on the great plated steel beams tying the upturned keel overhead. 'The arching of the roof, with enormous rafters stretching across it, possessed my fancy with ideas of Noah's Ark,' said Mackintosh, about the 'Basilica' which he had earlier visited in Vicenza, in Italy. He hadn't forgotten.

If not a great building, it is far from the conventional 1890s solution to the given architectural problem, full of quirky and often fascinating spatial as well as decorative detail. Look at the pendants in the gallery balustrade (and the capitals below), a motif CRM would develop to maturity in the Art School library over a decade later. Even if not stopping for a cup of tea, note the trusses in the roof-lit hall.

The next year, Mackintosh designed a Mission Hall in Ruchill Street, again for the Free Church. A short walk west along Maryhill Road from Queen's Cross, it stands – in grey rather than red sandstone – now rather lonely in the desert of Glasgow's destroyed street architecture. It is a small building, with interesting if simple shapes on the façade (eyebrows and nose surround windows to the right of the door). The main hall is top lit, which focuses on the elaborate cross beams.

Having not been appointed to design the adjoining church, which followed three years later, Mackintosh never built another church. Although he did design elements inside at least two others; a pulpit, a communion table, an organ case, light fittings and other decoration for a church near Stirling in 1904 and also for another (in 1905-6), which has since been demolished, in Paisley to the south-west of Glasgow.

Door detail at Queen's Cross Church

WINDYHILL

Although there are no genuine CRM houses in Glasgow, there are two real ones within commuting distance down the Clyde. To the south is Windyhill, at Kilmacolm in Renfrewshire. Please note that this is a private residence with no public access. To the north of the broad Firth of Clyde, in Helensburgh, and still easily accessible from

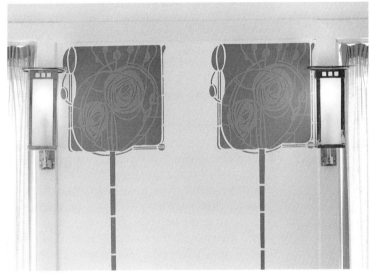

central Glasgow by suburban railway, is The Hill House.

Windyhill (1899-1901) might be seen as a step on the path to the considerably larger Hill House, built a few years later, at over twice the cost. It remains, however, an extraordinary achievement itself. Windyhill is Mackintosh's first essay in the sculptural massing of forms within a vernacular tradition, all unified (and dematerialised) under a cover of harling – Scottish roughcast. More important is the beautiful refined calm in its interiors, not overwhelmed with the 'rose boudoir' decoration of earlier Mackintosh interiors.

At Windyhill we see CRM's separate worlds of outside and in. The vernacular, unassuming and traditional exterior seen from the gate (1899), and the modern, artistic and delicate interior in the bedroom (1901).

HOUSE FOR AN ART LOVER

The House for an Art Lover, of course, was not a real commission, but an ideas competition, set by the interior design magazine *Zeitschrift fur Innendekoration*, which the Mackintoshes entered in a hurry in 1901. Though they didn't win (perhaps because their entry was incomplete), the set of drawings was published by the competition sponsor in 1902 as beautifully produced and subtly coloured lithographic plates.

The building completed nearly a century later in Bellahouston park is not a Mackintosh work. Inspired by the original drawings of CRM, it was realised by John Kane and Graeme Robertson (up to 1990), under Andrew MacMillan. It operates as an international graduate study centre for the Glasgow School of Art, a conference and function centre, high quality café and design shop.

The competition brief dictated the main spaces and also their size. Internally, we have here a memory of Windyhill, with touches of The Hill House (though that was designed later), writ luxurious and oh so large within an historic country house form. If you know the stair at The Hill House, the one in the hall here is like a giant's version – although the overall size is not that much more; all the details seem quite overscaled. Interestingly Roger Billcliffe has questioned if CRM would ever have wanted to build a house on this scale. The sadness is not that he didn't build this, but that its successful publication, known across Europe and in the USA, didn't lead to any other real architectural commissions.

The cavernous north-facing hall, with its low, enclosed gallery where facsimiles of CRM's published drawings are now displayed on a lectern, leads, through simple sliding doors, to the vaulted, comparatively low, but still overscaled dining room. This severe space, with its simple, strong-grained oak and its stone fireplace (virtually that in the Art School's first board room) is, like all the public rooms, well crafted. Many of the details are beautifully recreated: fireplace, furniture, lights and decorative panels, all in the forms of a Mackintosh country house.

The Ladies' Room is elegant and intimate. Right next door is the spectacular, long music and reception room. With the decorative panels by MMM in every window bay and each side of the piano at the

end, indeed with the constructed piano no less extraordinary but considerably less ornamented than as drawn by CRM, the richness does not dazzle, though the space may overwhelm.

What must impress here, more than spatial ingenuity, is surface decoration, detail and elaboration. To a visitor, therefore, it feels not unlike a visit to a stately home: except there is something peculiarly nouveau here; fleeting senses of Disney cannot easily be avoided. Cecil Beaton would have used these spaces as sets for 'My Fair Lady'. Glasgow's new image of itself would love nothing better. In its first months of opening, it was already selling itself in 1997 as a key attraction and one of the city's most popular venues.

The House for an Art Lover, built 1989-96 based on CRM's (1900-1) competition sketches, and within its own garden in Bellahouston Park.

THE HILL HOUSE

The Hill House is Mackintosh's domestic masterpiece, now in the care of the National Trust for Scotland. It is a fair walk from the seafront up the hill to the plot which his client bought in 1902, five minutes above the upper station from Glasgow, and among the prosperous mansions of Upper Helensburgh. Almost next door, there already was an Arts & Crafts house by Baillie Scott (who had won a prize in the Art Lover's House competition); nearby were others by more local architects but mostly appearing equally English – with foreign whitewash, half-timbering and lots of red-tile roofs. The client 'put to Mackintosh such ideas as I had for my prospective dwelling. I told him that I disliked red-tiled roofs in the West of Scotland with its frequent murky sky; did not want to have a construction of brick and plaster and wooden beams; that, on the whole, I rather fancied grey rough cast for the walls, and slate for the roof; and any architectural effect sought should be secured by the massing of the parts rather than by adventitious ornamentation. To all these sentiments Mackintosh at once agreed... My wife and I were shown over a house he'd designed at Kilmacolm, and left convinced that Mackintosh was the man for us.'

The house recalls the Scots 'baronial', in outside image and even more in plan; but we need not chase its origins in a fusion of the conventional Edwardian north-corridor house (the west half), and a seventeenth-century Z-plan Scots tower-house (to the east). Simply approach this stately, solid house, clearly rooted in its place; knock at the dark door, absolutely plain apart from a square of nine small square lenses of clear glass; and enter.

Through an inner screen that is really a glazed thick trellis, and before rising four steps into the main hall, to the right is the door of the library. This is the client, Walter Blackie's study, lined with

◀ *The hall of The Hill House with clock, chair, carpet and light fitting designed for it in 1903-4. Influences from Japanese architecture to a classical Greek frieze are subsumed into a quintessential Mackintosh interior space.*

dark stained, grainy oak bookshelves and simple, rather Arts & Crafts, detailing; note the metal butterfly drawer-pulls. But the door's four, long, purple inserts of sparkling handmade glass had already intimated a less than conventional room beyond; and sure enough CRM offsets the conservative order with tiny inlaid squares of white enamel and purply-blue coloured glass, broken into by an occasional, single curving reed climbing the bookcase. This tall room is kept low by the oak fittings whose surrounding top rail at 8 ft (2.5 m) links together fireplace with its little windows, door and all the bookcases between. Then the southern window bursts upwards through this frieze, just like CRM's own studio at home. Mr Blackie would receive visitors here; it is the last of the world outside; only family and close friends penetrate further.

Looking up the four steps into the hall gives the feeling that we are still outside, in the public realm of getting and spending; that there is another threshold to be crossed before arrival at the heart. The progression deeper from the dark entrance towards the softest white at the house's heart centres on this hall and stair, on those intermediate spaces between the black and white. Once again CRM holds two extremes in dynamic equilibrium: one is seen in the hard shell, characterised by the adjectives strong, sober, empiricist, objective; here as at Scotland Street School, Windyhill, or even the School of Art, it is essentially a variant on the vernacular, on tradition. At the other end is the white interior, which attracts adjectives such as soft, decorated, idealist, fantastic, erotic; and this is essentially creative and modern – as in the School of Art director's room or the Mackintoshes' own living space. Here at The Hill House the actual outside shows one extreme; the deepest interior space, the master bedroom, the other. Of the other main rooms, the library tends to the dark (more traditional in its finishes and its decoration

▶ *Baronial elements at The Hill House (1902) belie a very different interior. CRM proposed a square garden divided into nine squares, but this never materialised. Mackintosh's only traces on the landscape are in the semi-circle up to the door, and the balancing rose-garden on the opposite side. As you circle the house, wonder at the changing satisfaction of its form, every view offering delightful, asymmetrical but tightly controlled compositions.*

as well as more sober); the drawing room tends to the light. Halls and stair mediate between the masculine, rather dour, tradition-conscious public world, and the feminine, almost dreamlike, fantastic and freely creative private world.

The lower hall appears ahead as a palely lit clearing in the dark forest through which we now approach. Note to the left, between the dark verticals, a shadowy hidden seat (under the upper

stair) from which we could be observed entering. Moving forward, solid and void uprights divide the dynamic space; tiny flashes of pink glass embedded in wood pass the eye. Turn left to climb; first four more steps and then turn the other way into the cool, north-lit stair drum. We run our hands across the open hall timbers as we do forest trees, not as the sensual sculpture in the white room ahead. These are structure: strong, expressive, dark beams and posts and planks for stair ballisters. Though explicit and constructive, this is no Arts & Crafts exercise in honest carpentry; it is symbolic rather than vernacular.

Through the frame at the head of the stair, six

little squares of glowing leaded glass in the dark door invite us into the Blackies' bedroom. Indeed all round the house tiny accents are made by touches of colour, of glass, of ceramic, of mosaic; used like lipstick or ear-rings, only in the places you are close enough to touch. The door opens and we enter an ivory mist. (Not only is the other

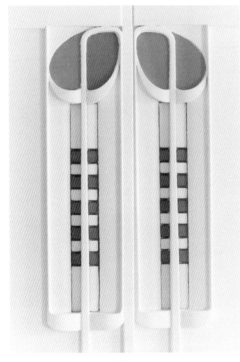

side of the dark door now white, but its little glass squares are enamelled pink inside.) Here materiality is disguised; wooden furniture is abstractly curvaceous, smoothly feminine and thickly lacquered in an ivory white – an extreme contrast to the structural clarity of stained timber in the library. The bedroom has an overall sleekness. With the material and carpentry obscured in the absence of a workman's touch, it is all sensual surface – curves, sharpness and extreme subtlety of form.

Note, however, how precisely the room is formed. The bed recess is beautifully contained under a low barrel ceiling. The shallow, enclosing vault springs from wardrobe doors on one side and from a gentle bow, echoing the vault itself, on the other. This bedside space bellies out to one tiny, low window at its centre. Here the whole thickness of the protective bedroom wall seems scooped dangerously thin; it is a riskily exposed moment in this womb-like, enclosing place. Safely thick little curving, interior shutters, each with three milky pink glass squares in them, when opened admit the morning sun to hit the pillow.

Mackintosh intended this intimate vault to be separated by gossamer veils edged with bejewelled glazed screens. That would leave two spaces; first, the dressing area: under the light fitting and in front of the tall mirror between the two windows. The symmetry of the mirror between the windows is balanced by a tall, ladder-back black chair between the twin wardrobes, which appear to reflect the window forms as negative solids of space. The second space, the fireside ingle, links to this, held by the enclosing band formed by the line of light fitment, window-head and wardrobe-tops. Here the built-in settle opposite the washstand snuggles into the wall thickness, the seat's top aligning with the fireplace.

Onto all this geometric order, built up of cubes and the two shallow cylindrical curves, a veil of decoration is layered. All the ivory walls are most delicately stencilled as a rose bower in mauve and green; between the wardrobes the roses climb through the black grid of that trellis-backed chair. This frieze is uninhibited and light, in contrast to the more polite and formal beauty we will see in the drawing room below. Flower heads fly, and long leaves blow like hair in the wind. Here is a nudity not of masculine structure, as in the stair hall, but of sensual feminine surface.

The strangely curved, smooth, ivory-lacquered shapes set off the naturally coloured materials – the pewter water jug, untreated fabrics, mirror, or enamel and pinkish tiles, the extraordinary, sharp luxuriousness of naked, polished sheet-steel with inlaid mosaic roses around the fire. In this deepest interior of the house, all hint of historical reference or vernacular has vanished. The freshness and yet sensuality is very far from its contemporary, the cloying, entwining continental art nouveau.

Before leaving, note the small white table. It is

◄ *In the principal bedroom, two ivory wardrobes flank an austere black ladderback chair which stands in front of a frieze of informal roses stencilled on the wall. This balance of geometric and organic is seen in detail on the double doors of each wardrobe. Elegant botanical abstraction against patterns of squares, all in milky pink glass and layers of thick lacquered cream paint. (Not being allowed to touch, we must take on trust the stunning visual effect of looking through these doors when open against the sunlight.)*

square topped, with four legs more like leaves than stems, paper thin but curving down, facing each other diagonally, and joined by a little square timber with four square holes cut from it; that geometric description belies the extreme elegance of this delicate, dynamic and satisfying object. Leaving the bedroom, we are gently squeezed by the narrowing of the ogee curved door jambs, out of which are cut little rectangular niches for a flower vase at face level.

▶ *The stairlight is built of a structure of nine cubes. The four corner cubes of this open-work metal cage, which contain the light bulbs, are each glazed on all four sides with a cube of nine little leaded glass squares It is one of CRM's most remarkable forms, not least in that we can only see it by spiralling round it as we descend, from looking down on it to its being right above us.*

Glance next door, into the one other sober, masculine space (where the dark woods and simple purple highlights are in a similar language to the library). This is Walter Blackie's dressing room at the top of the stairs; then, next to it, note the wash room with its wonderful shower, perhaps the first such shower in Scotland, where horizontal jets spurt from a cage of chromed copper pipes. In the dressing room don't miss the exquisitely simple mirror in front of the window; the square in which Blackie framed his face and his day's first thoughts, the open rectangles to the sides framing the Arts & Crafts red-roofed neighbour. Also, note how CRM wraps, with an explicitness and quiet irony, a heavy mahogany wardrobe round Blackie's antique chest of drawers.

In the upper hall note the inglenook, the little 'seat-room', up two steps, low ceiled, and enclosed with arms, as if in the thickness of the wall. Anne Ellis (the National Trust's former custodian) calls this alcove a 'sit-ooterie', after the half-secret spaces where a girl could safely sit out a dance but yet remain on the edge of the ballroom floor. The Hill House has many such rooms within rooms, or rather such edge places, half in and half out of rooms, which revel in the playfulness of such ambiguity. They are natural spaces for children, who so instinctively enjoy these boundary games as well as the changes of scale.

In the second bedroom opposite, look at the drawings originally deposited with the Dean of

Guild for building permission, now exhibited (in facsimile). Note on plan how the billiard room would have been, and how the drawing room music bay has changed; and how, further along this corridor are other bedrooms and the hidden ways up to the wonderful children's world. (We can only imagine the effect of its glorious window when looking up from outside, unless we hire it for a holiday flat from The Landmark Trust).

Much of the house was finished and filled quite conventionally; and more bedrooms have recently been opened to the public. But Blackie gave CRM complete control of library, main bedroom, drawing room and hallways, including cabinets and cases, chairs and clocks, carpets  and wall decoration. A large proportion of this is carefully in place (often restored or, like carpets, replaced) today.

On the way back downstairs, note the stair light, another of CRM's most remarkable objects; it epitomises his geometric concerns at The Hill House – and it can only be seen by moving diagonally past. At first it is below eye-level, its form revealing itself as we spiral down underneath it. Down into the hall, we are surrounded by Mackintosh's metamorphosis of a classic frieze, the triglyphs and metopes of the Greek temple. The expressive metopes are here squares of pale blue stencilling, with pink and black checkerboard patterns and one carefully placed touch of green. The triglyphs between, articulated strictly geometrically, framed in dark oak, are sets of three tall thin strips of pale purple enamelled glass. Its essence is a balance between the extremes emphasised in the rooms we have already seen, these opposites of tradition and modernity, dark and light, nature and artifice, masculine and feminine, yin and yang.

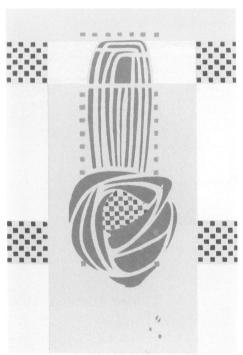

From this evenly north-lit platform, a dark door with six glowing little opal white squares opens to the most brilliant distant view: every visitor must draw breath on opening this door. Directly ahead, a glazed rectangular bay, diminutive under a lowered ceiling which acts as the brim of a cap, captures the stunning panorama across the distant water of the Firth of Clyde to the south.

Detail of the wall stencilling in the drawing room, a more formalised wrapping than in the bedroom, based on patterns of seven squares among the abstracted roses.

As ever Mackintosh's strictly geometric armature here carves three-dimensional spaces with precision. To the left another small rectangle is cut in the wall. Darker than the window space ahead, and similarly separated by the horizontal planes, this space is for music. The room, therefore, is graduated from the winter fireside to the garden, via the music alcove, which with its own little window and window seat is also a tiny room within a room. The window bay is a bower, slightly mysteriously enveloping as we approach. It is surprisingly deep, a real little summer room, with its own threshold layers: through the wall thickness, across the light strip, to reach the little columns which define the seat space. There is a sense of fragility, of vulnerability, stepping into this space – we have broken through the great solid harled mansion wall, we find glass down to our feet on both sides – and yet we are safely held close. Note the delicate white columns, opening into stylised flower petals at the head,

which frame the seat; little geometric panels of pink and green leaded glass, across which bends a single blue-ish reed, are high on the white panelling, pink leaded glass inset in the ceiling above.

The main rectangle of the room is held within a light, encircling band unified by a low cornice which forms the door and fireplace head and the ceiling height of the music alcove and the window bay. Below, a trellis of white and shiny silvery stripes decorated with pink roses, pale green foliage, and occasional falling petals, catches and throws the light differently as we move. Above, the space rises another metre; the shape, disappearing into darkness, is ambiguous, for both

The music 'room' and the window 'room' extend beyond the drawing room. When CRM was asked to replace his ceiling mounted lights in this room he fitted the lower wall sconces which remain.

walls and ceiling are the same deep damson. (At least it should be; when the wall lights replaced gas fittings which had dropped from the white ceiling to the rail height, CRM finally specified a dark, low-gloss 'plum' sheen. Having been painted a dead black for many years it is currently 'restored' to CRM's first, pale proposal – though the original drop gas lights are not reinstated. Where, as here, we know of various extremely different decorative

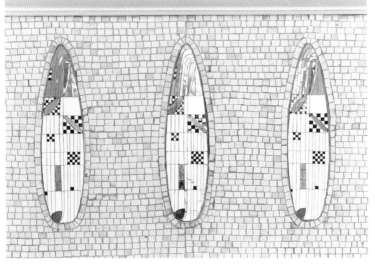

Detail of drawing room fireplace mosaic.

schemes by CRM, conservation proposals become an unusually interesting topic for argument!)

The slightly concave fireplace, with its mosaic surround and oval mirror inserts behind the fire irons, holds a fine gesso panel by MMM. Note the shelving unit to the fire's left, with its central plant and branching pink glass leaves at each shelf; and look at the window opposite, whose edges are ever so slightly curved into the room, with seven little pink glass squares and a longer slit beneath, mediating between light and dark.

All the movable furniture, like the beautiful cabinet at the end, between this window and the fire, is dark, stained or ebonised. (This cabinet repays close inspection. See how the glass doors are subtly curved and angled; note also the little decorative triangles in the centre below these doors, the motif, also used at the same moment on Scotland Street school, which so dominated CRM's later pattern-making.) In counter-point to the little table we saw in the bedroom, a small black table stands in front of the bay. This key piece, made for the room in May 1908, is a geometrically pure essay in squares. Its formal austerity is melted, as ever: the centre of the top has four mother-of-pearl inlaid squares, each of which actually consists of nine tiny squares, set with their grains at right angles to each other, thus catching the light differently as we move past. Just as the white table in the bedroom was not entirely feminine, but softened from a conceptual, formal armature, so here, the rigorous, abstract, black geometry, is centred on this delicate, feminine, natural patina, its surface fleeting with our changing viewpoint.

Before leaving, see the very different dark, panelled dining room, where Mackintosh incorporated the Blackies' traditional Edwardian values. Antique furniture and silver stands alongside CRM's sober bronze and white glass shapes on the window-wall and magnificent gas light fitting over the table, where deep purple encloses a white glass interior.

Notice how CRM's yin and yang of composition, material and form, has been intimated almost subliminally, in the stencil pattern just inside the front door. On the threshold between the public and private worlds, the porch decoration is a very simple stencil: the shadow of a flower curves across a checkerboard ground, (we see the proportion 5:8:13 which, in Fibonacci's series, tends towards golden section). It sums up Mackintosh's desired dynamic balance. His aim was the nurturing of a modern life, which could be protected within society by a strong, masculine shield; one whose goal, within this nurturing eggshell, was 'sweetness, simplicity, freedom, confidence and light.'

TEA ROOMS

Catherine Cranston more or less invented the Glasgow tea room phenomenon. She filled the need for a miniature social centre which served many purposes: to be a safe meeting place for bourgeois men in a city famed for the evils wrought by drink; but more, it uniquely offered 'ladies' rooms' where respectable women could go out and meet, at a time – over a century ago – when women without men in the urban scene were usually taken for servants or prostitutes. These were not cafés, but offered a range of privacies in the public world; rooms for lunch or private dining, rooms to read and write, to play billiards or smoke. They were almost clubs without bedrooms; and, centrally of course, without alcohol. Kate Cranston had avant-garde taste, and became the Mackintoshes' most stalwart patron.

Though CRM had earlier done a mural for Buchanan Street and furniture for Argyle Street, the Ladies' Luncheon Room for Cranston's temple to temperance in Ingram Street was, in 1900, the Mackintoshes' first complete tea room interior. Designed for the (16 ft 6 in / 5 m high) ground floor space in Miss Cranston's block, it was rebuilt for the Mackintosh exhibition in 1996.

The end bay held the silver-walled entrance corridor and stair; a low screen in which are set glazed panels separates this entrance from the lunch room where, once seated, over the lobby we see the great curvaceous panel (14 ft 9 in / 4.5 m long) entitled *The Wassail*. This is CRM's work, and parallel, on the opposite side wall appeared its partner, MMM's *May Queen*. Both these vast artworks went to the Vienna exhibition of 1900.

On the other sides were a back gallery and, opposite it, the window wall which was handled as a space of its own. Double depths of column at the street, with a high-level rail binding the inner columns, marked each window bay as an

◄ *The last and most remarkable Cranston tea room was The Willow. Here the most complete space is the Room de Luxe (1903). The room is encircled by a deep band of dissolving complexity at eye height. The long side is a range of windows, each inset with silver mirrored hearts (seen from outside on p53). The other sides are ranges of mirror inset with panes leaded in purple and pink glass. (Silver chair backs with inset pink glass squares can be seen mirrored in this image.)*

individual place, with its own banquette seat and facing black, tall-backed chairs.

As restored for the exhibition, in 1996, we notice how the screen – the alternating leaded glass panels below, of pure, abstract vegetable designs simply in translucent pale pea, black and white – doesn't fight with the extraordinary richness above – vast panels of gesso on hessian and scrim, the bejewelled and beflowered ladies formed with twine, glass beads, thread, mother-of-pearl and tin leaf. Between them, little drop-lights, so simple and yet so beautiful, give a golden down-glow reflected in the saucer above and the fireworks on its sides. This wonderfully restored interior is part of an on-going project to restore all the tearooms for future display.

The most remarkable of the Cranston tea rooms was the last in the series and the only one which partly remains and is partly in use today: The Willow. Here CRM remodelled the facade and amended the structure as well as carving out and linking the interiors. With the theme from Sauchiehall, which is said to mean 'street of the willow', the interior design was built around lines of Dante Gabriel Rossetti:

'Oh ye, all ye that walk in Willowwood
that walk with hollow faces burning bright...'

The willow tree and its leaf are behind all the imagery, often abstracted to an extreme, as seen in two ground floor elements: first, the lattice back of the curved settle which, separating front and back diners, was the order-desk chair (now in the Art School), and second, the extraordinary plaster panelled frieze round the wall (discussed on p68).

The ground floor front and back saloons, and the top-lit mezzanine gallery at the back, made three interrelated but distinct places. The street front, in silver, white and rose, was the Ladies' Tea Room; the dark Luncheon Room for men and women was behind; the Tea Gallery above, a rose-bower in pink, white and grey. Then, on the first floor, overlooking Sauchiehall Street, was the

Ladies' Room, a silvery willow grove, the exquisite 'Salon de Luxe'. This Room de Luxe was entered through glazed double doors, the most simple and straightforward in form, but now among the most famously decorated doors in the world. Further up, behind windows whose section above the encircling doorhead rail was deeply recessed (forming lovely, low window bays), were found the dark stained and panelled Billiard and Smoking

Rooms, with motifs of applied squares. In the basement (and actually next door), shortly before the First World War ground to an end, CRM added another room, 'The Dug Out'.

The Willow Tea Rooms façade detail, showing the 'fenêtre en longeur' (the room-wide window) of the Room de Luxe from outside.

Two rooms, the back gallery and Room de Luxe, were reopened in 1983, after extensive restoration by Geoffrey Wimpenny (of Keppie Henderson, descendant of Honeyman, Keppie & Mackintosh). So today we enter through Henderson's, a jewellery and gift shop of trinkets and uncontrolled reflections. The top-lit back gallery, held on great steel joists, has the eight tapering columns (note their capitals); there once were, also, vertical rows of more tiny squares; symbolic trees simply supporting the ceiling grid of enclosing foliage.

Further up we reach the Room de Luxe, until a few years ago entered through magnificent glazed doors. The shapes and colours of their leaded lights can entrance the eye for hours; to see them swing as waitresses bring through the tea-trays, and how different they look from different sides and in different lights! (These doors were removed to travel with the 1996 exhibition, and were to be

back in their original and everyday – their extraordinary and exotic and magical – use. But their fragility has made that hope unrealistic; instead, replicas will be in use at the Willow Tea Rooms, and the original doors will eventually be displayed there.) They remain CRM's most elaborate essay in stained and leaded glass.

Here the chairs today, in their aluminium paint, seem stage props, clumsy reproductions; yet in fact the originals, silver-painted and upholstered in purple velvet, were very similar. (Originally only eight of these tall chairs stood at formally aligned central tables, surrounded by others with lower backs. Today's scatter and randomly placed tables offers a quite different spatial sense.) The colour scheme of silver and purple, while feminine, has moved on from CRM's white rooms designed in the year or two before: and the space is architecturally, rather than decoratively composed.

The elegance is held by the precise spatial control: the low cornice at doorhead onto which rests the barrel ceiling is a rail which runs all round, holding together the lower walls of mirrored and leaded panes separated by thin white vertical bands, below which the walls were upholstered in pale grey silk, stitched with beads; the banquette seat backs in purple velvet. The vault comes down to the low street windows, each casement with its hearts of silver mirror. The endlessly reflective complexity dissolves the edges of this stylised grove into the distance. Only the high flat cap of the fireplace and, opposite it, of the frame for MMM's gesso panel based on the Rossetti sonnet just touch the ceiling's barrel, breaking the implied lowness of the space, down to which the groups of four-square light fittings drop. (MMM's gesso, *Oh, ye that walk in Willowwood*, like the doors, was exhibited with the 1996 Glasgow exhibition and has not yet returned home. It also may end up as part of a display elsewhere within the building.)

Originally a central chandelier was made up of myriad rose-coloured glass baubles on strings surrounding a large bulb. It has long since vanished. That's a pity, for seeing it, and other details from this interior, like the strings of glass balls in the balcony edging which are preserved at the Hunterian, would make us wonder how close we are sailing here to the tawdry.

On opening in October 1903, the Willow interior was an immediate *cause célèbre*. It is strange to imagine this fairy place of pearls and roses as purveyor of teas, scrambled eggs and mutton pies to everyday Glaswegian folk. An amusing contemporary tale by my aunt's father, Neil Munro (written for the *Glasgow Evening News* at the time) charmingly encapsulates an ordinary pair's first experience of this 'Room de Looks'. In the end, 'when the pie cam' up, it was jist the shape o' an ordinary pie, wi' nae beads nor anything Airt about it, and Duffy cheered up at that, and said he enjoyed his tea.'

◀ *Looking through the wonderful glazed doors into the Room de Luxe (1903). Today the light fittings visible beyond are very similar to those CRM used widely elsewhere, from his own house to the Ingram Street Ladies' Luncheon Room. Of the original fitment which hung centrally in the Room de Luxe, with its drops of pink glass, Neil Munro's Duffy asked: 'What are all these drips and dangles?', to which his companion replied: 'Airt, that's Airt.'*

SCHOOLS

CRM designed two schools; the first, Martyrs' Public School (1895), when he was Honeyman and Keppie's assistant in charge. It closely resembles the plan and organisation type of the conventional small board schools of its time. If you could get inside (and it is now in public ownership, though probably to remain in use by the Museums

conservation department), Martyrs' would show the typical educational environment of a century ago. Symmetrical, with boys' and girls' entrances to east and west giving to the central hall, off which – and off its upper floor galleries – are three layers of conventional classrooms. CRM's signature is suggested by the art nouveau motifs around the entrances, and on the timber eaves which fly out over the stairhead windows. The overall form is rather clumsy and boxy. Internal details, restored and refurbished, add touches of charm: the metal balustrade brackets, the wall tiles, the glazed wooden screens.

It is really only in the roof trusses, and especially

Above: the early Martyrs' School. Opposite: one of the soaring stair towers of Scotland Street School (1906), showing the extraordinary, daring precision of masonry and glass, under its conical slate hat.

▶ *The centre of the south façade of Scotland Street School, seen from the playground at the back, but designed ambiguously like a front. This articulation of form, the plasticity of red stone and shadow with spots of green glaze (centring on an abstract thistle symbolising Scotland), is one of CRM's most unprecedented and satisfying surface treatments.*

the six closely spaced trusses over the stair, which seem pegged in a Japanese manner, that the designer's character shows through. Here we learn a little more about Mackintosh: for during renovation work which removed plaster from the stair head, it became clear that the pairs of brackets which seem to hold the truss ends, as if pegged to the ends of double beams, are merely short decorative additions. The visible structure is interesting timberwork; but some other interesting timberwork is simply meant to look like structure!

Mackintosh began to design the Scotland Street School in 1903; it was completed, 25% over budget, in 1906. The planning, as with all CRM plans, is absolutely within the given tradition. Two great stair towers on the front (one over the boys', one the girls' entrance), flank the hall above which sit two layers of classrooms. The vast vaulted cookery room at the top, where a 23 ft (7 m) long dresser and a cabinet by CRM remain, fills the length between the stair towers; it is worth the climb. Seen from the front, thinner, stepped layers of cloakrooms are next to the stair towers, with staff rooms at the outer ends. On the back, absolutely directly, we see three layers of six classrooms, each with three windows. Only minimal decoration (including some green-glazed surfaces) articulates the centre and end bays with abstract, geometrical tree and thistle.

This ambiguity of front and back – the classically symmetrical southern side, the stair towers and other additive bits to the north – is played quite faintly. Moreover, while the curving glazed towers suggest the winding stair of the traditonal Scottish country house, here the plan is quite different. Straight flights and landings stand back from the bay, leaving great semi-circular wells of light between outside and in. Inside these towers, note the spare, elegant joinery above, the metal ties, circles and rods; and once you're up there, enjoy the magnificent view north across Glasgow.

The central hall is surrounded by white tiled 'windows' and blue tiled columns, all with green trim. Rather than being conventionally enclosed by walls, this space is articulated by sinking the hall four steps below the main noisy thoroughfare of children, and beyond a row of piers; by having side bays on the ground floor between deep fins (like theatrical boxes); and by the columns set back from the mezzanine balcony edge. All this creates a wonderfully useful theatrical space.

For the rest, the magic is in the detail. At the entrances, note how CRM, mannerist as ever, has classical details drape over the porches like tasselled tablecloths. Then look up at the pinched peaks of the masonry columns under the attic storey. The decorative treatment at the significant places of the building – entrances, stairs and where it hits the sky – shows CRM now at his most abstract. As you leave, note the formal composition of the caretaker's house; look at the wall and fence, in such elegant daring masonry and metal; and see the pattern of almost square shapes on the railings: an abstraction of thistle seeds, symbolising the children as Scotland's future.

THE MACKINTOSH HOUSE

There are no original houses by CRM left in Glasgow. Hous'hill, Miss Cranston's home, was destroyed, the Mackintoshes' own house demolished. But the latter is rebuilt, using genuine interiors, within the University of Glasgow (Hunterian Art Gallery) Mackintosh Collection; while a House for an Art Lover has recently been constructed in Bellahouston Park.

So, as chimerical as the tea rooms, the domestic interiors of Mackintosh have had a remarkable ability to dissolve and reappear in front of our eyes. Even the room which 'The Four' created for the Vienna exhibition in 1900 was reconstructed in Edinburgh in the 1980s, but as soon vanished again.

The Mackintosh House in the Hunterian Art Gallery brings us, through various veils, to how they lived ('they', for it is as surely the result of MMM's sensibility as CRM's alone). Rebuilt only a few metres from its original site, most of the interior we see here – the actual fitments, from freestanding bed or sideboard to the fitted fireplaces – had already been moved by the Mackintoshes themselves, from the Blythswood Square flat which they had fitted out on their marriage in 1900.

Contemporary photographs of that earlier flat show the fine classical Glaswegian drawing room, transformed. The space was emptied of late Victorian clutter, and lowered by an enclosing rail. This ran along walls and, where it crossed the windows already diffused with taut white muslin, it dropped translucent veils embroidered (we guess) in pale purple and/or green. Narrow gas pipes are taken in decorative loops across the ceiling from the central rose to wonderful drop fittings in the corners, softly to illuminate the whiteness. The walls are panels of grey canvas against each of which stood one important designed element: fireplace, desk

◄ *The drawing room (recreated as 1906). Interior architecture is the great synthetic art. Its popularity a century ago created cluttered, fin-de-siècle jungles. But CRM cut through the confusion. Here the enclosing rail lowers the Victorian window-head (to the left) and ties in the new window (to the right) which he cut in the gable wall 'for my wife Margaret, so that she can watch the sunsets.'. Onto the refined spatial order, CRM layered surface detail of coloured glass, fabric, embroidery or stencil; and then the moveable pieces which altogether complete the design.*

or bookcase. The dining room is smaller and almost like a shrine, with its wall candles, dark wood furniture and walls lined with coarse, dark wrapping-paper. The white bedroom, though spatially insignificant, is filled with organic forms decorating the white furniture offset by coloured glass; here was the elegant foundation of CRM's European fame in those next few years.

All this came with them when they moved in 1906 to Gilmorehill and thence to be rebuilt in 1981. Today, entering the typical, narrow and tall hall of this mid-nineteenth century terrace – from the Hunterian, as we must – you see the inside of the front door, with its four square lenses, the panelling bellying out towards the reformed window and mirror opposite, held together by the dark framing at door height – all touches aimed at widening and lowering the sense of this tunnel. Simple austerity is offset by the petal wall lamps (which had been exhibited in The Rose Boudoir in Turin in 1902). Before passing, look again at the large mirror, designed for their own use by MMM (with her sister and brother-in-law). This strange design in beaten lead, the first and last view of themselves at the point of transition to the public world, represents what? With its peacock tails above and below, but even more the fish leaping in front of bearded profiles mirrored left and right.

Next door, the small dark dining room is muted; dull walls clothed in a black trellis with stylised pink roses are offset wonderfully with silver drops of rain, or cherry blossom in a wind. Windows and door seem left untouched. The dark chairs (first designed as architectural bodies shaping places in the Argyle Street tea rooms) complement the table and sideboard which the Mackintoshes designed for themselves.

Upstairs, we open the only door, small in scale and inset with 20 of the loveliest pink glass tears (though we really only see their quality from the other side), to enter the L-shaped room, looking

▶ *The dark-painted and virtually unaltered dining room. The focus is on the dining table, which would have been laid with CRM-designed silver-ware and lit from CRM-designed candle-sticks. The room builds a subtle palette of browns with (out of the picture) the dark trellis and CRM fireplace, set off by spots of silver.*

through from the cool studio to the sunnier glow of the drawing room. As theirs was the end-of-terrace house, CRM could create a long first-floor window in the south-facing gable wall; this, and the removal of other doors and partitions on this floor, transformed it into a quite unexpected place.

The mood here is an utter contrast to that below: a white, spacious calm fills the space. The wall between the two rooms is pulled up to stop at the band which runs round the entire area at door-head. This band, so close above the head (and appearing very differently from the many low-angle pho-tographs often p u b l i s h e d) frames and en-closes the space r e m a r k a b l y, while also extending it hor-

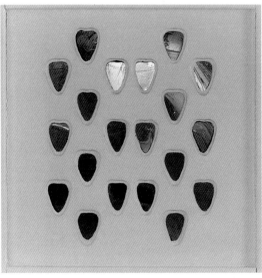

Detail of the door to the first floor room, whose colours change as you move past and the door moves open.

izontally. Where it runs across the tall study window, this band offers translucent pink and purple squares; where it runs across the drawing-room's typical Victorian bay window, a wall drops down to it, tightening the horizontal geometry of the room (and creating of the window bay an extraordinary place to be in!). The high window representing 'studio' is not just a conversion necessity: exactly the same device is used to repre-sent 'library' at the new-built Hill House, where the window rises above the enclosing rail. Of the other windows, the rail forms the heads; particu-larly the new long set of small-pane, leaded casements, which, quite differently from the large pane Victorian sashes at the front, attract the body to approach, open, and look out at Gilbert Scott's romantic university turrets.

The division of spaces down to a rail at door-head is a powerful Japanese domestic tradition. While CRM may have seen memories of this in Smith & Brewer's Mary Ward House in London (1895), no contemporary designer articulated it as he did. The potentially linked Art School studios show one extreme; this subtle restructuring of the first floor of his own home is brilliantly convincing. Light floods into this space, diffused through muslin, to show up the many remarkable objects and elements within. These are all well described for visitors, but any can repay close attention. I will mention a very few.

In the studio is the yin and yang pair, the bookcase and writing desk. On the white, low curvaceous bookcase (of 1900), its sinuous plants and tear drops in front of the four full moons is a particularly subtle essay in leaded stained glass. As with the 1902 drawing room cabinet next door, the material just happens to be wood; the luxurious, curvilinear surfaces mask inevitably difficult wooden junctions under thickly lacquered paint. The black writing cabinet, standing with its doors open (like an open kimono) is its dark, geometric twin. Designed for Hill House in 1904, the original is perhaps the masterpiece among CRM's furniture. This is the copy which CRM-MMM had made for themselves. Here luxury is in the material, which is not hidden. Woods are carefully chosen and revealed, the mother-of-pearl squares of squares, the formal geometry, is always softened with tiny touches, with ivory and with the central metal panel decorated eloquently (and differently from The Hill House original) with the crying rose in leaded glass. These two pieces are wonderfully complementary, but they also show just how CRM's designing had moved within those few years from the 1900 style which brought him

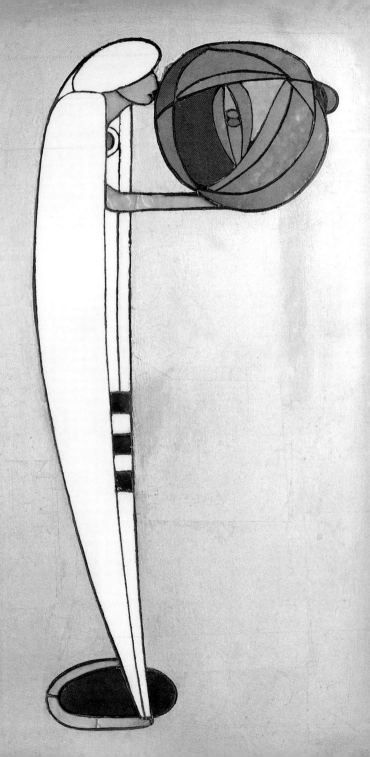

instant fame to the controlled maturity of 1904.

Above the fireplace stands MMM's gesso (plaster) panel called *The White Rose and The Red Rose*. Look closely, for no photograph does justice to this delicate richness; the face, the beads, the scrim, as it catches this pale light.

Through to the drawing room, look at the white desk, and the doors on its front, with women and roses, as ever, on MMM's silvered copper panels. Note the exquisite tiny circular table in the corner; thickly lacquered, brilliantly shaped, and easily overlooked. These are indeed sensuous surfaces. As Alan Crawford rightly notes, 'visitors wait until the attendant looks away, and then touch them,

stroking the silky surfaces as they would stroke a lover, exploring, looking for reassurance.' Today CRM's objects, designed to enrich their users' everyday experiences, are transformed into museum valuables and we must resist the temptation to make contact with them! But look even more closely at the forms; how sections change as they rise from the floor (the dining room chairs were also a good example), or how the support of the weight of table-top or cabinet is expressed.

There is no warm clutter; no patterned wallpaper, upholstery or rugs. We might contrast this turn-of-the-century interior with the National Trust

Opposite: drawing room cabinet doors (1902); the stylised woman and rose may have been formed by MMM in coloured glass on the silvered doors. Above: MMM gesso panel above studio mantelpiece.

for Scotland's 'tenement flat', on Garnet Hill, only two minutes' walk from the Art School (a typical, small petit-bourgeois flat of the same moment). In the Mackintosh house all is Art. Yet it is not extravagant – it is very often the cheap luxury of cream paint and coloured glass and enamel. But it is also of purity of space, simplicity of form, economy of means, as in the aesthetic dried flower arrangements.

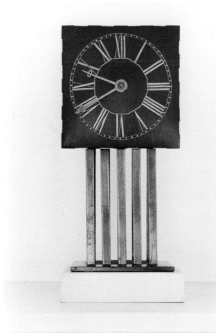

Going up one more flight, we recognise the stairhead plaster panel placed here by CRM; it is from the frieze back in place on the ground floor of the Willow Tea Rooms. Of these panels (from 1903-4), Nikolaus Pevsner said, 'he discovered the necessity and possibility of abstract art in his wall panels several years before Picasso and Kandinsky had begun their efforts to liberate art from nature.' Perhaps this panel is indeed where we can best apply art historical terms like 'pioneer' to Mackintosh. The category of being 'first' doesn't seem very useful in approaching an artist's work, least of all CRM, whose goals were quite different. But here the date is important. Perhaps I find the panel incongruous here because the rest of this house was built of ideas (and indeed of many physical bits) which are a few years older; CRM of the Willow and The Hill House had been moving on from the home he was here recreating with MMM. The tale

The tiny clock (1905) on the mantelpiece in the drawing room; a version of one designed by CRM for The Hill House.

of this panel as liberating abstraction is, however, more ambiguous. For CRM's drawing of the frieze shows it coloured, decorated and filled towards the top with densely packed pink roses. (Ah, says Billcliffe; but in making it, CRM resisted what was 'almost certainly Margaret's influence and tendency to apply pattern and decoration to every square inch.') A fine work of art, as always, offers a silent mirror to the viewer, in which to see his (in these

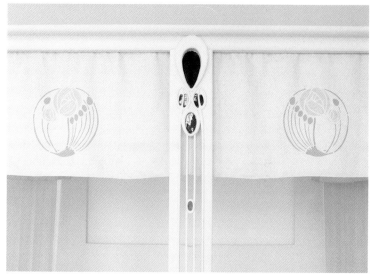

cases) own views of Modernism, sexism or whatever.

Detail of the first four-poster bed CRM designed, for his marriage to Margaret Macdonald in 1900.

On the second floor, the partition is again removed and a smaller L-shaped room results, formed by its architectonic objects – the fireplace, the cheval mirror (the very one which was in the room setting in Vienna in 1900) and the great bed designed for their marriage in 1900, (all of which came from the Mains Street flat, all capped at the same height, of an upstretched arm).

Note the tiny glass lenses on the central bed-end, which, in the morning sun, cast coloured light onto the bed. Look here at the beautiful birds (are they doves?) on the wardrobe, their claws stretching down to form the handles. See the carved plant motif on the tables, as they run down to the floor at the corners of the legs; and again look at the gorgeous lights: orange glowing within brazen cubes of metal with a tear drop in each side and their enclosing saucer above.

Having failed to get to the attic bedroom up the smaller stair with its surprising black and white vertical striped wallpaper, we try the bathroom door and are astonished to find ourselves in the gallery, a bizarre and tall new space. We have moved from a Mackintosh space to the world of exhibited artifacts. The Hunterian holds over 600 Mackintosh drawings and designs, as well as 30 important pieces of furniture, and else besides including work of MMM and their twin couple in The Four, her sister Frances and husband Herbert McNair (whose son donated many of the items, from the Mackintosh estate).

So here is exhibited a changing collection of furniture, drawings, banners and paintings. There are touches of the decorative layers of the Willow Tea Rooms – chequered and willowleaf pattern leaded glass panels (set high up in the walls to the left); and fragments from the balcony edge – sparse, flat steels with square punched holes and thin bent rods with green glass drops and vertical strings of glass balls.

Often on display, and worth looking for, is an absolutely stunning table, in mahogany and with a pearl dot drawer handle, designed in 1912 for his friend William Douglas, who as a decorator had worked on various CRM projects. Its eight, elegant, aerofoil legs stand four in corners and four between the spreading spokes halfway to the centre. At the centre, these spokes rise into a tower lattice with its very 'constructional' (half-notched) joints. This is as subtle, complex and satisfying as the 1908 cube table at The Hill House, and much less well-known.

In addition to this scatter of exhibits, here is also

▶ *Derngate guest bedroom (1919). The geometric decoration almost turns the room into one four-poster bed. With their severe forms, enlivened just by the grain, black edging and ultramarine stencilled chequers and the squares of mother-of-pearl on the handles, these oak pieces were made by German prisoners-of-war on the Isle of Man in 1917.*

the complete guest bedroom from 78 Derngate: dazzling black, white and ultramarine stripes (in a tiny room), which frame the simple oak furniture. The bedside chest, with six little drawers, five long ones and a top-opening cabinet, is a perfect engineer's tool box! When on one occasion Bassett-Lowke's guest George Bernard Shaw was asked if the jarring decoration in this room hadn't disturbed his sleep, Shaw replied that it was no problem. He always slept with his eyes shut.

Having descended again, the abiding image of this visit to the Mackintosh house is of the drawing room and studio; that white space. Did Margaret really paint her etiolated gesso maidens while wearing kid gloves, standing on a white carpet? In this world which 'cannot tolerate an intrusion of the ordinary' (to quote Hermann Muthesius, their key contemporary German supporter and friend), where is the space for everyday life?

Yet that question might seem strange to a Japanese, from whose culture CRM took such inspiration. In Japan, not only are restraint, subtlety of form and surface, and economy of means prized, but the flower arrangement or the bowl on the table are as much art work as the paintings on the wall. In our era of 'minimalism' as high taste this is far from news; but in Glasgow a century ago it was revolutionary.

INFORMATION DIRECTORY

Properties Open to the Public

Glasgow School of Art, 167 Renfrew Street, Glasgow G3 6RQ. Still a working Art School; access by guided tour only, April-September, daily, seven times a day; October-March, Mon-Sat, twice a day, access via Dalhousie Street entrance. The best time to get a fuller view of this building in use is at the annual exhibition of student work in June. (It may be totally closed the previous week for external examinations.) All dates and times are worth checking in advance. Tel: 0141 353 4526; www.gsa.ac.uk

Queen's Cross Church, now headquarters of the Charles Rennie Mackintosh Society, 870 Garscube Road, Glasgow G20 7EL; open Mon to Fri 10am-5pm; and Sun 2-5pm, March to October only. Admission charge. With the co-operation of all those involved with the Mackintosh heritage, the CRM Society is able to arrange guided tours – write or telephone for details. Tel: 0141 946 6600; email: info@crmsociety.com; www.crmsociety.com; www.mackintoshchurch.com

Ruchill Church Hall, Shakespeare Street, Glasgow G20 9PT. This busy hall, not far from Queen's Cross Church, is open for viewing Mon to Fri 11am-3pm; Closed July and August; enquire at the Church House in the courtyard. www.crmsociety.com/ruchillchurchhall.aspx

Windyhill, Kilmacolm, is not open to the public and can only be seen from the public road.

The House for an Art Lover, Bellahouston Park, Dumbreck Road, Glasgow G41 5BW; exhibition, café and design shop open daily 10am-5pm, admission charge, due to private events times may vary, telephone or check website for details. Tel: 0141 353 4770; www.houseforanartlover.co.uk

The Hill House, Helensburgh, Strathclyde, G84 9AJ, approximately 23 miles NW of Glasgow; just over a mile uphill from Helensburgh station (up Sinclair Street, over the railway by the Upper Station, then left into Upper Colquhoun Street). Owned by The National Trust for Scotland. Open daily April to October in the afternoons, 1.30-5.30pm, although access is restricted at peak times, and visitors may have to wait until others have left. Tel: 01436 673900. www.nts.org.uk

Willow Tea Rooms, 217 Sauchiehall Street, Glasgow G2 3EX. Open for light meals and tea during normal shopping hours. Tel: 0141 332 0521. www.willowtearooms.co.uk

Ingram Street Tea Rooms. The Chinese, Oak and Cloister Rooms have now been partially restored by Glasgow Museums, following the example of the beautifully restored Ladies' Luncheon Room, which went on tour with the CRM 1996 Exhibition.

Miss Cranston had opened a tea room at 205 Ingram Street in 1885 and by 1907 had acquired the whole block, 205-217. CRM designed a number of interconnecting rooms, beginning with the Ladies' Luncheon Room in 1900. In 1907 he added an Oak Room, fronting onto Miller Street. Like the Ladies' Luncheon Room, this too had a double columned space at the street; but unlike it, this one carried a gallery, inevitably blocking light from getting deeper into space. In 1909, he designed the Oval Room and Ladies' Rest Room; in 1911 he designed the Chinese Room. Here there was a dark ceiling hidden by a bright blue horizontal lattice, square trellis work and deep strong colours. Up till 1911, CRM had used colour very sparingly. Suddenly we have bright blues and reds on black; it is dark and exotic. The next, and last room at Ingram Street, the altered Cloister Room of 1912 is quite different again. This low barrel vault (which hid an earlier CRM decorative scheme) had layered wall panels of shiny, waxed wood, decorated with delicate vertical strips of harlequin lozenges painted red, green and blue, and with much mirror glass round its low vault. There are what look like round-headed double doors (or recessed panels?) covered in thin strips of leaded mirror under an extraordinary, melting doorhead. Was this a totally new, restless space developing from the recently completed Art School library? When we see this mysterious room restored, our view of Mackintosh surely changes. Here was a quite different exoticism, a taste of cosmopolitan Vienna.

The Argyle Street Tea Rooms may have left us only furniture; but the amazing range of interior spaces from Ingram Street survived. They were closed in 1949 and bought grudgingly by the city in 1950 (under pressure from Thomas Howarth and others). The building had become an unloved, tawdry, tartan souvenir store when I was a student, cruelly called 'The Charles Rennie Mackintosh Discount Warehouse'. The interiors were finally removed and stored in 1971. Glasgow Museums wouldn't take responsibility, and neglect led to scandalous decay. Finally Glasgow began making magnificent amends, and with the help of Heritage Lottery funds, sections of the Ingram Street Tea Rooms have now been restored, and parts of the Chinese, Oak and Ladies' Luncheon Rooms are currently on public display in the Kelvingrove Art Gallery and Museum.

Kelvingrove Art Gallery & Museum has a Glasgow Style gallery with exhibits from the Ingram Street Tea Rooms, including furniture, amidst other work by CRM and his contemporaries in Glasgow. For current information telephone Glasgow Museums, 0141 276 9599 or visit the website www.glasgowmuseums.com

Scotland Street School, 225 Scotland Street, Glasgow G5 8QB. Closed as a school in 1979. Since 1990, The Museum of Education, open all year, Monday to Thursday, and Saturday 10am-5pm; Friday and Sunday, 11am-5pm; admission free. Telephone: 0141 287 0500. www.glasgowmuseums.com

Martyrs' Public School, Parson Street / 11 Barony Street, Glasgow G4 0PX. Saved in 1970s by public protest from demolition. Restored for Glasgow Museums; it is currently closed while a decision is made by Glasgow Council regarding its future use.

The Mackintosh House, Hunterian Art Gallery, University of Glasgow, Hillhead Street, Glasgow G12 8QQ. The Mackintosh Gallery has changing exhibitions. The reserve collection holds up to 800 sheets of CRM drawings, including flower drawings and related material, to which access is available by appointment. Open Mon to Sat, 9.30am-5pm. Confirm opening times in advance; telephone: 0141 330 4221; www.hunterian.gla.ac.uk

Properties not Illustrated:

140-2 Balgrayhill Road (1890). CRM's first known work; very ordinary semi-detached houses designed for relatives.

Craigie Hall, 6 Rowan Road, Glasgow G41 5BS. Designed by Honeyman (1872) and extended by Keppie and his assistant CRM. Detailing on the doorcases and in the library (1892-3) is probably CRM's; the music room and organ case (1897) certainly are. A professional office not normally open to the public.

Queen Margaret Ladies' College (1894-5). Queen Margaret Drive. Designed by Keppie with CRM; redevelopment planned for a hotel, apartments and homes.

Glasgow Herald **Building** (1893-4), Mitchell Street. CRM's first big architectural job; a simple newspaper distribution warehouse whose only particular requirements were a water tower (important fire precaution) and a clear route through the middle of the ground floor for dispatch vans. For the idea of the corner tower, CRM returned to his storehouse of travel sketches and, on blank sheets in his Italian sketchbook of 1891, he made the first sketch designs for the *Herald* tower. On the most prominent corner,

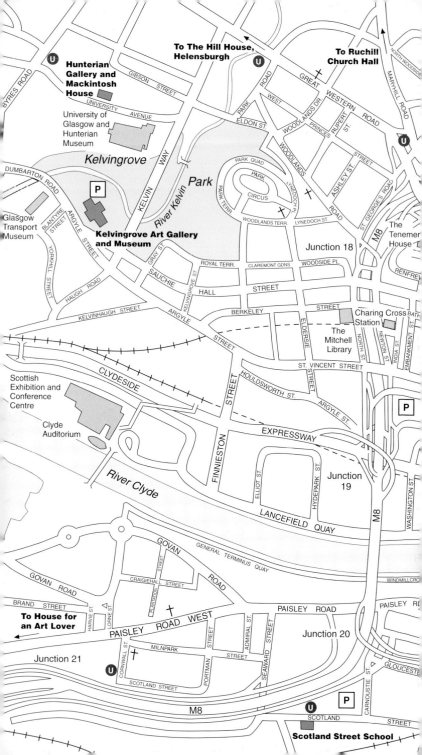

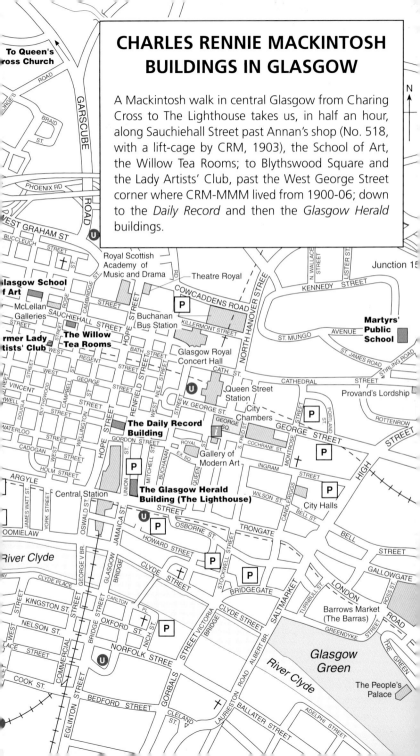

CHARLES RENNIE MACKINTOSH BUILDINGS IN GLASGOW

A Mackintosh walk in central Glasgow from Charing Cross to The Lighthouse takes us, in half an hour, along Sauchiehall Street past Annan's shop (No. 518, with a lift-cage by CRM, 1903), the School of Art, the Willow Tea Rooms; to Blythswood Square and the Lady Artists' Club, past the West George Street corner where CRM-MMM lived from 1900-06; down to the *Daily Record* and then the *Glasgow Herald* buildings.

the tower is dramatically visible; the stonework on the facade is well worth a close look. The visitor centre for the building has been taken over by Glasgow City Council. For further information contact Glasgow City Council; www.glasgow.gov.uk

Daily Record **Building** (1900-1) Renfield Lane. A conventional warehouse and print works, CRM's effort being concentrated on the surface to this narrow lane. It is clad in white glazed bricks. If this is presumably to increase reflected illumination, that will help only the opposite neighbours. For CRM it is a play on image, as ever; here the image is that of the enclosed light-well of Edwardian blocks (which never appear on an outside!). The ground floor, however, is a grey sandstone arcade; the undulating heads very minimally formed and exquisitely precise, the shapes of capital, keystone, arch, implied most economically – apart from the doorway whose mannerism is a brilliant play of forms, thrown away down this narrow lane.

Looking upwards, the bays of the surface are articulated simply; the dotted green bricks topped with red triangles, as stylized trees, carry the eye up to the sky, where we glimpse a great cap of stone waves and a baronial turret!

The Lady Artists' Club (1908), 5 Blythswood Square. See how CRM stuck a wonderful black classic portico in a round-headed entrance. He also worked in the hallway and ground floor of this now private office.

An Artist's Country Cottage, uncommissioned project published by CRM in Germany (1902); recreated from these drawings 90 years later at Strathnairn, 7 miles south of Inverness.

78 Derngate, Northampton (1916 and later), is a small terraced house remodelled by CRM in 1916-1919. The properties at 78 and 80 Derngate were acquired to conserve the buildings and open them to the public. No. 80 has been transformed into a visitor centre and exhibition space, while the interiors and exteriors of No. 78 have been restored in careful detail to the original CRM schemes, including the paint finishes, wallpapers, textiles and carpets. Open February - until last Sunday before Christmas, 10am-5pm. Last entry 4.30pm, closed Mondays except Bank Holidays. Tel: 01604 603407; e-mail: info@78derngate.org.uk, web: www.78derngate.org.uk

Gourock Parish Church, down the Clyde, south-west of Glasgow, has an indifferent pulpit and choir stalls by CRM (1899).

Holy Trinity Church, 12 Keir Street, Bridge of Allan, Stirling.

Pulpit, communion table and organ screen (1904), richly carved in oak in CRM's unique, organic Gothic exuberance. Usually open on Saturdays 10am-4pm, between 1 June and 30 September; telephone 01786 832093 or 834155.

Selected Books on Charles Rennie Mackintosh

Overview: Fine story, up-to-date scholarship and good value for money: *Charles Rennie Mackintosh*, Alan Crawford, London, 1995 (paperback); *Charles Rennie Mackintosh*, essays edited by Wendy Kaplan, Abbeville Press / Glasgow Museums, New York and Glasgow, 1996. Best for your coffee table: *Remembering Charles Rennie Mackintosh*, Alistair Moffat, Colin Baxter, Lanark, 1989; *Charles Rennie Mackintosh: Synthesis in Form*, James Steele (words) and Eric Thorburn (photographs), London, 1994. For ideas: *Charles Rennie Mackintosh: The Poetics of Workmanship*, David Brett, London, 1992 and *Part Seen, Part Imagined*, Timothy Neat, Edinburgh, 1994. For a story of his life: *Charles Rennie Mackintosh, Architect, Artist, Icon*, John McKean and Colin Baxter, Edinburgh, 2000.

Glasgow School of Art: Five studies, quite different and not all equally accessible: William Buchanan (Ed.), *Mackintosh's Masterwork*, Glasgow, 1989; Robert Harbison, 'The Glasgow School of Art: Master of Building', in *The Architects' Journal*, 14 June 1989, and Mark Girouard, 'The Glasgow School of Art', in Kaplan (editor) 1996; James Macaulay, *Glasgow School of Art*, London, 1993. *GA49: Glasgow School of Art*, Japan, 1979, with a brief essay by Andy MacMillan.

The House for an Art Lover: *Charles Rennie Mackintosh*, Meister der Innen Kunst 2 – Haus Eines Kunstfreundes, Verlag Alex, Koch Darmstadt. The published document on which the new House for an Art Lover was recreated. A modern facsimile of this original portfolio of drawings with text in English by H. Muthesius is in print, but not cheap. On the other hand, the complete set is well reproduced in Steele (see above).

The Hill House: John McKean, 'The Hill House' in Kaplan (editor) 1996; James Macaulay, *The Hill House*, London, 1994; *The Hill House*, NTS booklet with text by Roger Billcliffe (and Anne Ellis).

Tea Rooms: Alan Crawford, 'The Tea Rooms: Art and Domesticity', in Kaplan (editor), 1996; Perilla Kinchin, *Taking Tea with Mackintosh*, San Francisco, 1998. For a wider context see this author's *Tea and Taste, Glasgow Tea Rooms 1875–1975*, Oxon, 1991.

Scotland Street School: Gavin Stamp, 'Scotland Street School: Master of Building', in *The Architects' Journal*, 6.4.1988.

The Mackintosh House: Pamela Robertson, *The Mackintosh House*, Glasgow, 1998, is an exquisitely beautiful souvenir of the building.

Painting, Furniture and Collaboration

This guide to CRM's spatial and built designs has only mentioned moveable works where they are accessible in Glasgow; therefore it has not focused on drawings, paintings or furniture in themselves. They are well covered in key references.

Painting: Roger Billcliffe, *Charles Rennie Mackintosh, Architectural Sketches and Flower Drawings*, London, 1977 and his *Mackintosh Watercolours*, (3rd ed) London, 1993; Pamela Robertson, *Charles Rennie Mackintosh: Art is the Flower*, London, 1995.

Furniture: Roger Billcliffe, *Charles Rennie Mackintosh, the Complete Furniture, Furniture Drawings and Interior Designs*, (3rd ed), London, 1986.

Textiles: Roger Billcliffe, *Mackintosh Textile Designs*, San Francisco, 1993.

Margaret Macdonald: Her particular contribution is well contextualised in Jude Burkhauser (editor), *The Glasgow Girls*, Edinburgh, 1990.

Biographical Note: John McKean was born in Glasgow and studied architecture at Glasgow School of Art. He is Professor of Architecture at the University of Brighton, and is the author of three books on Charles Rennie Mackintosh.

Index

THE PROMS
and Natural Justice

A Plan for Renewal

ROBERT SIMPSON

Foreword by
Sir Adrian Boult

Published by
TOCCATA PRESS
1981

First published in July 1981
© Robert Simpson 1981
All rights reserved

ISBN 0 907689 00 0

Photoset by AGP Typesetting Ltd., London SW18
Set in Garamond 11 on 13 points
Printed and bound by the Thetford Press Ltd., Thetford,
Norfolk

CONTENTS

To my friends in the BBC

FOREWORD

by

Sir Adrian Boult, C.H.

As well as his widely known music, especially his symphonies and string quartets, Robert Simpson is also the writer of scholarly books on Nielsen, Bruckner and Beethoven. His long experience as a BBC producer from 1951 to 1980 has enabled him to watch closely the various ways in which the Henry Wood Proms have been run, and I suggest that all who are interested in this great annual festival and its future should read this book and come to a decision about it.

Dr Simpson rightly maintains that it is morally indefensible that one person, no matter who it is, should control the planning of the Proms for an indefinite length of time, and he proposes, not that there should be a return to the old committee method, but that the Prom planner should operate for a limited time. He also demonstrates carefully that a great deal of money could be saved if the various BBC orchestras were to take over most of the concerts. This would be good both for the orchestras and for the BBC.

For the sake of consistency in upholding the principle involved, the author has felt it necessary to decline a Prom commission for a symphony. His views must be taken very seriously.

THE AUTHOR

ROBERT SIMPSON was born in Leamington, Warwickshire, in 1921. Initially intended for medicine, he discontinued his studies after two years to study music. After studying with Herbert Howells, he took his D. Mus. at Durham in 1951. In 1952 he joined the BBC's Music Division where he worked for nearly thirty years until his resignation over cultural policy in August, 1980.

One of Britain's foremost composers, Dr. Simpson's impressive output includes seven symphonies, eight string quartets and many other works for various combinations. The Robert Simpson Society was formed in 1980 to further knowledge and understanding of his music — a rare tribute to a living composer.

He has written on numerous topics and is the author of *The Essence of Bruckner* (Gollancz, 1967), *Carl Nielsen, Symphonist* (Kahn and Averill, 1979) and the BBC Music Guide, *Beethoven Symphonies* (1970), and edited the two-volume Penguin, *The Symphony* (1967). He is the holder of the Carl Nielsen Gold Medal (Denmark, 1956) and the Medal of Honor of the Bruckner Society of America (1962).

PREFACE

'THE ROAD to Hell is paved with good intentions' is a slogan much favoured by defenders of entrenched positions; if the system they are operating suits them, and seems well oiled, suggested alternatives are usually dubbed impracticable. You make matters worse if you drag in ethics — the good intentions can then be represented as some sort of romanticism, not to be taken seriously. Yet most reasonable people will agree that ethics are involved in such matters as monopoly, dictatorship or totalitarian bureaucracy, and few will support the idea of absolute personal power. On the face of it we may wonder what these portentous remarks have to do with the much-loved and often joyous Proms; yet the person running them has untrammelled sway over the choice of a very large number of musicians, and over the musical fare of a vastly larger number of listeners. The fact that a single individual has the complete authority, virtually unrestricted in time or scope, to decide all this in detail, has been dangerous these twenty years, against the interest of equity, and therefore not morally defensible. A weak recognition of this is betrayed by the repeated plea that the planner takes advice, though the more frequent protestation, poorly substantiated, is that there is no practical alternative to the present method. It is my purpose to show such arguments to be sophistries, or at best imperfectly reasoned.

Having no personal stake in the matter, and never having had any wish to be involved in the running of the Proms in any capacity whatsoever, I hope the views expressed here will be judged for themselves. It is going to be necessary to insist tiresomely on the ethical question, for two reasons — first, that it is the basic spring of the argument, and second, that the BBC has hitherto consistently failed to reply to it.

1

All this will be made clear as the pages turn, as it is demonstrated that there is indeed a practical alternative to what is wrong, an alternative not only practical but positively advantageous, both artistically and financially. It is done, I hope, without heat but with some force. Frankness is necessary though at times it has to be tempered, as can be seen from the following clause of the contract I naively signed at an early age when joining the established staff of the BBC:

> The employee shall not either during the subsistence of this Agreement or after its determination for any reason disclose to any person firm or company in any circumstances whatsoever any information processes or secrets relating to any of the business or affairs of the Corporation which during the subsistence of this Agreement or after its determination may come to his knowledge but shall at all times keep such information secret.

While reassuring the reader that this little book is not written in that style, I must make it clear that certain aspects of the argument must be governed by the awesome phrase 'or after its determination'. That means till death (no problem after that, one assumes). Although I am no longer a member of the BBC staff, having resigned in protest at what seemed to me unacceptable cultural policies, I am still not free to say all I wish. The reader may wonder what the BBC has to fear from a mere musician; so do I — it is after all above reproach in the conduct of its business and must be quite without anxieties on that score. Such restrictiveness might be expected from the Ministry of Defence, the Ku Klux Klan, or the broadcasting corporation of some repressive state.

Be that as it may (and the BBC will come up with some depressingly plausible reasons), the reader will have to forgive the absence even in political asylum of disclosures of internal discussions arguments agreements disagreements actions business policies affairs intrigues plots mayhem cabals backstabbings free fights brawls or private fights. To disclose, I take it, means to reveal what is not known beyond a certain proprietorial circle, and so all the germane facts hereinafter mentioned are well enough known to need citation only for the benefit of those who may not know or may need reminders. There is a little essential history but alas no dirt. Nevertheless a number of questions must be asked; although I know the answers to most of them I cannot reveal these. But there is nothing to prevent me putting the questions on behalf of the reader, who is entitled (having paid for his licence) to seek the replies from the BBC. I would be most interested to hear the results, to see how they compare with what I know.

Having stuck obstinately to the point and harped on the principle to the end of Chapter 7, I had no wish to maintain the basilisk glare any longer; hence the less gladiatorial and more fugitive nature of the afterthoughts that prompted the last Chapter. But they are not irrelevant to the Proms, which exist to serve some of the needs they reflect, and they raise questions often asked by music-lovers who go to concerts. In contemplating the book as a whole, my first intention was to try to keep the first person out of it; but some effects of the contractual restriction, as well as the need to narrate from experience, made it impossible. I hope it has at least been prevented from becoming obtrusive.

R.S.
Chearsley,
June 1981.

1. THE PRINCIPLE

DEFENCE OF ethical principle has never been one of the more successful human activities. Even the great religions owe much of their success to other than moral persuasions; their record of resistance to ethics is undeniably impressive. Any large concern can point to similar achievements, in quality if not in scale, and this is the story, helped along by a parable or two, of a minor such triumph of the British Broadcasting Corporation. While perhaps only a few zealots in Broadcasting House might speak of the BBC in the same breath as Hinduism or Christianity, the Corporation is, like each of them, formed by the mores of the society it reflects, and while it develops dogmas it entrenches an establishment of its own. The dogmas tend to adjust to society and sometimes expediency; the establishment may seem to some entrenched and self-perpetuating. The dogmas of commercial organisations are governed by profit. But the BBC is a publicly funded service; any dogma it has is said to be derived solely from its aims as a service, and its regime purports to be the guardian of these. The principle optimistically defended and repeated without any apology in this essay is raised in connection with one of the Corporation's many activities — the Henry Wood Promenade Concerts — but it is basic to good human behaviour, and so inescapable in any field. There will be those who do not regard the Proms as of great significance in the largest human terms. To them I would say: think of the argument in terms of civilised morality applied to any situation you call important and you will see that it is an authentic principle. In this case it is of incalculable importance to a great many musicians and to millions of listeners. If the BBC modestly hesitates to compare itself with a great religion we might remind it, to begin with, that the Proms reach in one year an audience about one-seventh the size of Islam.

Before going into the awesome responsibilities thus entrusted by the BBC to one person (till death or retirement, whichever is the sooner, regardless of what you or I might recommend), we must tell how this came about. There are two recent histories of the Proms [1] and we can be content with recalling that when Robert Newman, manager of the Queen's Hall, started the Promenade Concerts and appointed Henry Wood their conductor, the case for or against personal monopoly was scarcely in dispute. No public body was involved, the scale was small, and Wood's choice of repertoire was for himself to conduct. There was nevertheless surely a number of musicians, composers and performers, who will have been unfairly neglected, perhaps unconsciously, and unable to get redress because everything depended on one man's decision. Newman died suddenly in 1926 and the Proms were in jeopardy.

The following year the BBC took responsibility for them and (with one short hiatus in 1940 and 1941) for their expansion ever since. But Henry Wood remained artistically in charge; he got help from Edward Clark and Julian Herbage, and despite evidence [2] that he sometimes found the BBC more than tiresome, he was never ungrateful for the rescue. The vastly increased audience put a heavier weight on his shoulders, but he was (and in my view remains) the only person ever to have had the right to bear it singly. He performed the whole of the Proms. It was his show.

From 1941 onwards other conductors began to share the load with Wood; the demands of their different interests brought a committee into being, and this assumed full powers after Wood's death in 1944. A committee is not usually the best means of achieving artistic ends. The stronger the tradition on which it is based, the more likely is it to stagnate. The regular pattern of the programmes had

[1] David Cox, *The Henry Wood Proms*, BBC, 1980; Barrie Hall, *The Proms and the Men Who Made Them*, Allen and Unwin, 1981

[2] Quoted in Cox, *op. cit.*, pp.109 *et seq.*

proved highly successful (a claim the BBC is not slow to make for its present system!); the regular nights for special composers had been the perfect way of familiarising the public with the great masters, and there were plenty of new works, slipped in here and there at opportune, strategic times. It was an easy system to operate, and a committee concerned with maintaining an accepted set pattern needs to vary it only gently each season. It is not surprising that the BBC committee became moribund and a sitting target for William Glock, the energetic new Controller, Music. He abolished it for the 1960 season and thereafter; the BBC was presented with a *fait accompli* and for the next fourteen years the Proms were in his hands.

This is the moment to make clear that this little book is in no sense a personal attack on William Glock or on anyone else. The fundamental issue is the essential morality of a method that, for reasons that seemed good to him and many others, he felt it right to institute. No-one but he can know how far he agonised over the ethics of continuing it indefinitely, and we must accept his good faith; many opinions have endorsed the brilliance and originality of many of his ideas and his productive enthusiasm. We are more entitled to question the vitality of the BBC's regime in the matter. But though we may have diverse views about the quality and nature of the Prom programmes, past and present, any analysis shown here is directed only at demonstrating the dangers of an indefinitely persisting control by one person, whoever it may be. These should have been obvious to the BBC when Glock's 'coup' was apparently not questioned, and even more obvious when it seemed later to be limply assumed that responsibility for the Proms rested automatically, constitutionally, on his successor. The principle is not concerned with the particular virtues or flaws of the individuals in the case. It maintains that since everyone has prejudices, the dangers may be mitigated only by changing the person from time to time.

Glock's transformation of the Proms is in any case no

argument for supposing it to be a panacea. As it righted wrongs, it raised (by default) the principle we are discussing; no matter how gifted or imaginative, how evangelistic for worthy causes, how inspired is one man, his idiosyncrasies and prejudices will feed themselves over a long period, try as he may to eliminate them. This is not a plea for another committee. Artistic conceptions are best from a single mind, prejudices and all. It is useless for the Controller, Music to surround himself with advice in the hope of evading the trap; if too much advice is taken the result will be a committee product, the proverbial camel; if the veto is too freely wielded the old hazards come back. 'Consensus' can only rarely be artistically imaginative. A group may prove effective if the aim is not too wide or complex, and provided individual originality is not stifled by corporate decisions. Purely scientific matters are properly tested by experiments in which many experts take part, but only the free single clear creative mind can generate artistic integrity. It is desirable that one person should do the work of devising a venture like the Proms, untrammelled except by practicality — but not for too long. *Tyrannosaurus reith*, the shrewdest of the dinosaurs, defined his ideal government as 'benevolent dictatorship tempered by assassination'. The moral appeal of such tempering is in no way improved by a natural urge to use it to mitigate the BBC's way of running the Proms, and it is fortunate that milder methods are available, less satisfying perhaps, but adequate.

William Glock himself (who in a note to me referred to our principle as 'perfectly legitimate' without enlarging on it) will forgive me if, before going any further, some statistics are offered. The easiest way to parry statistics is to say they can prove anything, that they are merely playing games with numbers. As will appear later, the predictable attempt has been made in our case. But statistics can represent human facts, as these do. They show without bias some effects of one person's unrelieved direction for 14 years of the programmes of 718 concerts containing 2911 items, heard by an audience of some 100,000,000 per year (taking into account the worldwide broadcasting and recording of the Proms). None of the composers mentioned is without a significant number of substantial admirers; the names are in alphabetical order. First, some who got nothing performed in those fourteen years:

Richard Arnell	John McCabe
Niels Viggo Bentzon	Ildebrando Pizzetti
Derek Bourgeois	Max Reger
Stephen Dodgson	Franz Reizenstein
Benjamin Frankel	Hilding Rosenberg
Berthold Goldschmidt	Franz Schmidt
Vagn Holmboe	Gerard Schurmann
Herbert Howells	Matyas Seiber
Kenneth Leighton	Nikos Skalkottas
Francesco Malipiero	Bernard Stevens
Frank Martin	

The reader will find others; this is not a 'loaded' selection and the composers are of various periods and nationalities. Here are some who got less than an hour's music done in the whole of this period:

Arnold Bax. . . . . 29 mins (2 works)
Richard Rodney Bennett. . . . . 51 mins (3 works)
Ernest Bloch. . . . . 20 mins (1 work)
Havergal Brian. 12 mins (1 work)
Alan Bush. . . . . 9 mins (1 work)
Ferruccio Busoni. . . . . 51 mins (4 works)
Arnold Cooke. . . . . 35 mins (2 works)
Aaron Copland. 27 mins (2 works)
Luigi Dallapiccola. . . . . 6 mins (1 work)
Peter Racine Fricker. . . . . 20 mins (1 work)
Alexander Goehr. . . . . 57 mins (3 works)
Arthur Honegger. . . . . 7 mins (1 work)
Elizabeth Maconchy. . . . . 16 mins (1 work)
Bohuslav Martinů. . . . . 29 mins (1 work)
Darius Milhaud. . . . . 32 mins (1 work x 2)
Anthony Milner. . . . . 40 mins (2 works)

Albert Roussel. . . . . 24 mins (1 work)
Edmund Rubbra. . . . . 19 mins (2 works)
Humphrey Searle. . . . . 32 mins (2 works)
Ronald Stevenson. . . . . 25 mins (1 work)
Karol Szymanowski. . . . . 27 mins (1 work)

In this case the number of works by each composer can be more significant than the total time occupied. If Bruckner had been represented by only one symphony he would have been an unlikely qualifier for the above list; we might mention that Henry Wood who, like most of his English contemporaries at the time, had no room for Bruckner, gave only one of his symphonies (No.7) during the whole of his reign (in 1903). The next one (No.4) had to wait fifty-five years. Until Glock's time Mahler was not much better off. A few cases quoted above need some comment. The two works of Bax did not include a symphony; one was a choral piece (*Mater ora filium*) and the other an orchestral arrangement of his oboe quintet! Honegger's only representation was, perhaps more predictably than it should have been, *Pacific 231*. Martinů's Sixth Symphony was due to the visit of the Czech Philharmonic in 1969. Milhaud's *La Création du Monde* cropped up twice. Like Bax, Edmund Rubbra was not represented by any of his symphonies.

But the purpose of this document is not to criticise programme details or to make out cases for neglected composers; it is simply to show how one man's policy can have far-reaching effects; no matter who it may be, similar symptoms will display themselves. The effects might be good or bad, or merely negative; whatever they are their undue prolongation can be only disadvantageous. Certain composers or performers (and performers are equally affected) may be thought not worth troubling about, or they may get crowded out by elements the Controller prefers. He can be unmoved by strong and informed advocacy, or by warnings. It is right that he should be firm in sticking to his views, but wrong that these views should be dominant for a time determined only by his age or health. Inconsistencies are inevitable under any regime; one wonders if even William Glock could explain why he included Delius in every season from 1960 to 1969, then dropped him altogether from his remaining four. Why was Rawsthorne included every year except 1969 while Rubbra got nineteen minutes in fourteen years, or Alan Bush nine minutes and Dallapiccola six? It is most unlikely that if the direction had been changed every three or five years the inequalities would have been so drastic. As Tovey said, time is not wall-space, and all composers cannot expect to get equal shares of it. But if it is agreed that the present system has self-evident and unacceptable perils, the claim that there is no practical alternative must be closely examined.

2. PRACTICE

THERE IS always a practical alternative to what is wrong. If the principle is seen to arise from a sense of natural justice that can be gainsaid only by sophistry we must, with the experience of working in the BBC, see what could be done to implement it. We must begin by explaining how the BBC Music Division came to have a Controller in the first place. The historical facts are not unknown but there will be readers unfamiliar with them.

Music was originally a Department and as such it had a Head. It was a 'supply' department; that means that its function was to supply programme material to the planners, the Controllers of the networks, especially the Third Programme and Home Service, on which serious music was regularly broadcast. It would normally submit three months' programmes at a time; the Controllers who paid for them would decide, after discussion, what to accept. Proposals could be heavily modified according to the judgment of various meetings and the availability of funds. Most artists were well apprised of the system — rightly, so that they could make realistic approaches.

In many respects the BBC is very like the Civil Service, placing great emphasis on hierarchical matters, in the field of structure as well as where persons are concerned. A Department is inferior to a Division (it is a section of one); a Division has to have a Controller, who is senior to a Head. The BBC executive presumably came to the conclusion that the administration of music in the Corporation would have greater prestige and perhaps greater weight with the musical profession if the Department were promoted from its status as a 'supply' section of Entertainments Division; if it became a Division in its own right, with the compulsory Controller. There is magic in titles and the BBC revels in them (there was once a DIRECTOR OF THE SPOKEN WORD, as well as a Department with, if I remember rightly, the sinister title SCRUTINY, where all scripts were vetted for contentious or advertising matter, and there was even a person known as MWYWO, which cryptic device stood for MUSIC WHILE YOU WORK ORGANISER).

The change might have made a stronger impression if the appointed Controller had been a distinguished musician. Richard Howgill, who was transferred in 1953 from the post of Controller, Entertainments to the new one of Controller, Music, was a gentle and modest man who would have made no such claim for himself; he was an experienced BBC administrator with a working knowledge of music, and was installed over the existing Head of Music, Maurice Johnstone. Howgill was seen, publicly as well as by the staff, to relieve Johnstone of matters distracting from artistic thinking, at the same time being responsible for wider policy decisions, or for negotiations with management or outside bodies. He naturally took an interest in, but did not greatly influence, the studio and public concerts of the BBC Symphony Orchestra; in practice these were in the hands of a producer in consultation with the Head, but the producer had great freedom, as may be imagined from a telephone conversation with Sir Adrian Boult:

> R.S. I'm just ringing to see if there's anything you'd like me to put in the next series of studio programmes I'm getting down to. I'd like to know now, so as to work round the things you want to do.
> A.B. That's your job. You put it down and I'll conduct it.

The perfect radio conductor! Discussions with Beecham were a little less relaxed. But the producer was still expected to make his own direct suggestions as they occurred to him, and to absorb the reaction ('You never heard such a bloody awful noise in all your life!' — Sir Thomas on an enthusiastic proposal of Berlioz's *Symphonie Funèbre et Triomphale*). The baptism of fire for this young producer was in fact thirteen concerts with Beecham and the BBC Symphony Orchestra, the first experience of production work, and (to mix metaphors) with a practically free hand to boot. We learnt the hard way: not knowing that Sir Thomas disliked being addressed through the studio loudspeaker, I ventured to observe through this medium that the second bassoon was not audible in one passage. In a voice that mere print cannot possibly suggest, he remarked to the orchestra: 'The British Broadcasting Corporation says it can't hear the second bassoon!' All this was before there was any Controller, Music, and Maurice Johnstone kept a fatherly eye on the lad, ready to jump to the rescue (he had once been Beecham's secretary and could usually cope with him with disconcerting ease).

In those days (1951-2) the Music Department did not have to supply the sheer quantity of music that is demanded now; the Third Programme was still young (born 1946), the envy of the world, deeply civilised in its intentions, and operating in the evening only. The department was somewhat smaller than now, and every music production was an event. Some of the programmes that now occupy the air as a stonewaller occupies the crease would have been rejected by the Third Programme either with contempt or as poor jests — especially the increasing number shorn of published details, with insensitive, disc-jockey-like removal of breathing spaces between speech and music, the bland superficiality of some of the smoother compères patronising to the intelligent listener for whom Radio 3 purports to exist. And the frequent replacement of concert intervals by brief and unspecified readings, however good in themselves, means that the production belt of classy aural wallpaper is the more relentlessly continuous. By such pseudo-commercial behaviour is Radio 3 losing more and more of its character as a general cultural service. A network of this kind cannot avoid a high proportion of good things, but the evidence shows that the Third Programme had a respect for the listener that is not now so rigorously upheld; this is the fault not of the music production staff (though it could do much more to fight philistinism) but the responsibility of the BBC's regime.

These matters may seem irrelevant to the Proms, but they serve to show that the first function of the Controller was seen to be only peripherally concerned with programme details and not to dominate the Proms; he chaired the committee and acted as honest broker or host. There was then, as now, a strong feeling at large that there was no real need for two people at the top; a single Head of Music had hitherto been fully able to cope, and there seemed to most musicians no reason that this was now not so. It must be emphasised that when the Department was created a Division there can have been no anticipation of increased volume of output; it was mainly a question of prestige, and the 'supply' function was unchanged. For a considerable time the same process continued, but with two heads instead of one. It was, moreover, widely known that the upper one had been appointed without advertisement, that it was a simple transfer from one job to another within the organisation. His two successors, on the other hand, were brought in from outside, again with no advertisement or visible process of selection. The BBC's apparent methods of managerial appointment will be considered in Chapter 5; the question has a bearing on the way the Proms are being run. With the appointment of Glock in 1958 the management did somehow contrive to provide the Division with a Controller who was also a musician of stature, but for all the public or the staff knew, this could have been pure accident.

Glock's advent changed everything. He seemed to agree with the idea that two heads were not as good as one and for a time (after Johnstone's retirement) he absorbed the Head of Music's post into his own. Besides his firm grip on the Proms, he had also personally adopted all the BBC's public music-making in London; this affected all the BBC Symphony Orchestra's programmes, leaving relatively little for its (by this time different) producer to do in the way of original long-term planning. But the daytime Music Programme drew more from the production staff, and it became necessary to restore the suspended post, re-named Head of Music Programmes (Sound). 'Sound' has become 'Radio' but the system, with minor changes still operates. Glock was succeeded in 1973 by Robert Ponsonby who, in the absence of any apparent management move to alter matters, inherited everything that Glock had personally arranged. Did the authorities forget (a) how a Controller, Music had come into existence and what his original duties had been, or (b) how William Glock had taken over the Proms? If so, their competence could have been open to question. Assuming their competence, we may reasonably ask how deeply they were concerned with the obvious dangers of the position.

It would be possible to extrapolate from Ponsonby's half-dozen Prom seasons (at the time of writing) in the way we have done from Glock's. But it would be neither fair nor altogether realistic. So far Glock is the only person to have made a complete demonstration of what happens if one person monopolises the Proms from appointment to retirement; under the terms dictated by the principle we are discussing, the figures from that whole period are meaningful. They would be much less so in an incomplete demonstration, though the reader might form an individual view of this or that lack, superfluity or just balance. It would perhaps be a little too much to expect Glock's successor to exude the same aggressive flair, to be possessed by the same urge to revolutionise the Proms, to have the same proselytising passion, the same bent to get rid of what he thinks should not be there. We have already noted that the stronger the tradition the more likely is it to cause stagnation, and the likelihood is increased the nearer we are to the tradition. History provides striking examples of the devastatingly crushing effect of some great masters on their immediate successors, and in such cases those who have been able to learn most from them have usually been original artists at many years' remove. The argument of not continuing an approximation to Glock's Prom pattern may well find support in other than ethical areas.

The view that the 'coup' of the Proms had its dangers was for a long time a topic of conversation among musicians, and in this case the military junta had not even promised free and democratic elections. Some (including myself) are now regretful at not having given earlier written expression to this disquiet; some members of professional bodies feel that it would have been better to approach the BBC long ago. Individual views may sometimes have originated in personal pique or disappointment and their expression inhibited by natural fears; more often, however, they were generated by thoughtful observation and a sense of fair play. In such situations action usually has to be precipitated, and how that happened is described in Chapter 6. In the meantime it seems reasonable to point out that it was not until Glock's control of the Proms had persisted long enough that one could speak of 'till death or retirement', and there was perhaps the ghost of a possibility that things might change. When retirement came it was finally clear that the BBC regime, like most such, was more interested in the *status quo* than in further revolutions that had not in any case even been proposed.

Later, when it was mistakenly supposed that Robert Ponsonby was 'under fire',[1] the BBC's defence was that Ponsonby took advice from respected colleagues. But no-one had assumed that a person running so vast an operation would do so without seeking advice and help, and the

[1] *The Guardian*, 15 July 1978, reporting the assertion of principle by the Composer's Guild of Great Britain in criticism of the single-handed monopoly of the Proms by anyone, simply because he was the BBC's music controller.

defence was not apt to the principle that was the sole basis of the criticism. The question was not properly answered, and no-one in the organisation seemed willing to discuss practical alternatives to a situation not admitted to be faulty. But it was nevertheless stated that any alternatives could not possibly be practical, and there was neither admission nor denial of the principle involved: if it were admitted, the search for alternatives would be mandatory; if it were denied, objections of impracticability would become irrelevant. Assuming the reader may admit the principle, let us see if the practical objections are insuperable.

We may readily suppose that Robert Ponsonby's instinct was not towards monopoly; indeed, before he actually took office at the BBC and was faced with planning his first Prom season while still managing the Scottish National Orchestra at Glasgow, he asked a distinguished composer to help him. This proved not possible; the composer was too much occupied with other things. Any arguments Ponsonby may have made for impracticability could well have been tinged with regret at not being able to implement what he might have hoped for. It would not be surprising if he thought the management might not take kindly to anything seeming to threaten a rise in the cost of the Proms — after all, a non-BBC planner might on the face of it be insufficiently aware of the need, for financial reasons, to make full use of the BBC Symphony Orchestra and its conductors, and unfamiliar with the way it is run; there could be some danger of the very expensive over-use of outside orchestras.

If the BBC were to take full advantage of all its own resources, this problem would vanish, as shown in detail in Chapter 3. A further objection could be that during the preparatory work many quick decisions have to be made. Programmes have to be changed for all sorts of reasons; such decisions can be made only by the Controller on the spot, not by somebody relatively remote. The BBC has a fully staffed concerts management with plenty of experience of the routines involved in concert-giving and expert in dealing with emergencies. The Controller, being on the spot, is able to work closely with these colleagues as his Prom plan grows; changes are effected with minimum fuss and delay. It could thus be argued that anyone planning would have to work in full-time consultation with BBC Concerts Management and perhaps also with the General Manager of the BBC Symphony Orchestra; it has even been suggested by a top BBC official that if the Prom planner were to be changed every few years it would be necessary to appoint a new Controller each time — as if Glock's change of direction were brought about by some sort off ineluctable natural force, or what the insurance companies refer to as an Act of God.

These difficulites are all amenable to the proper use of BBC resources, and in the next chapter we shall see how the Proms could be comprehensively planned a number of seasons in advance.

3. RESOURCES

...retrenchment could take two forms: less costly performers, or less enterprising programmes.

If you equate costliness with quality, and in the performing arts — by and large — you can, then the first alternative appears to mean a lowering of standards of performance; the second, a compromise over policy.

ROBERT PONSONBY in *The Listener*, 7 May 1981

THE REFERENCE is to what might happen if the BBC licence charge were grossly inadequate, assuming present methods of organising the Proms to be unchanged. The Fortnum and Mason approach to the question of costliness and quality will be dealt with in the following argument, but we must begin by proposing that proper advance planning of the Proms would be possible if they were mainly performed by the BBC's own orchestras; the chosen planner could give to Concerts Management a complete notional season founded on a far greater command of repertoire than before, and therefore wider in imaginative scope. Each series could be envisaged whole, and even each series of series. There could be purposeful streams inconceivable in the piecemeal compilations of the last twenty years. Wood was able to do something schematic by using one orchestra and a minimum of rehearsal; the strain was barely tolerable and the standard of playing hazardous. With five orchestras working all the year round in BBC time, there would be no lack of rehearsal, no serious fatigue problem and hardly any limits on repertoire.

To discover whether all this is fantasy let us take a cold look at the facts. The five suitable orchestras of the BBC are the BBC Symphony Orchestra (known in Manchester as the BBC Southern Symphony Orchestra!), the Scottish, Welsh and Northern Symphony Orchestras, and the London-based

BBC Concert Orchestra. The last frequently plays classical and romantic music of various kinds, sometimes very well, and performs studio operas to a standard depending on rehearsal time and the conductor's talent. It could further be used with minimal extra cost in combination with a regional orchestra for special kinds of works, rehearsing separately to a late stage. It might also be a source of extras. When at the end of 1977 I suggested that the Proms ought to be given largely by BBC orchestras, the idea met two off-the-cuff objections:

1. that it would be absurdly costly because of travelling and subsistence expenses, and

2. that the standard of performance would drop and the prestige of the Proms would suffer.

To counter the first criticism it is necessary to show the results of homework. The Prom season lasts eight weeks. Assuming that the Concert Orchestra would be reserved for an opera or two and otherwise for augmentation purposes, here is a comparison made at the time between actual costs of full symphony orchestras in the 1977 season and those that would have accrued if the BBC had used its own bands virtually throughout. The two London-based BBC orchestras incur comparatively negligible extra expenses and are not included.

(a)*1977 season*   £
British provincial non-BBC
orchestras (7 concerts)   34,623.17
London non-BBC orchestras (9 concerts)   71,653.90
BBC Scottish, Welsh and Northern (4 concerts)   13,050.52
Foreign orchestras (3 concerts)   21,700.00
                23 concerts   141,027.59

(b)*Notional use of BBC regional orchestras for 2 weeks each*
GLASGOW (68 players)   £
1. 14 nights' subsistence allowance @ £17 per head 16,184
2. 68 2nd class period return fares @ £26   1,768

(not allowing for group reductions)

3. Overtime for being away from base, assuming 5 concerts per week, averaging £36 per player   2,448

MANCHESTER (70 players)

1. As 1. above	16,660
2. 70 x £17.50	1,225
3. As 3. above	2,520

CARDIFF (66 players)

1. As 1. above	15,708
2. 66 x £11	726
3. As 3. above	2,376
30 concerts	59,615

Anyone fussy about exactitude may care to note that the last figure is 42.27187034% of the first total. If each orchestra were required to do two separate weeks (i.e., two visits to London with consequently doubled fares) the total cost would have been £63,334 (44.9%). Three visits, with three concerts on consecutive nights each time would obviate overtime and would have cost:

	£
GLASGOW	19.176
MANCHESTER	17.955
CARDIFF	15,642
(37.42%)	52,773

This last system would be both cheapest and best. The freshness of the orchestras could be better preserved. It would provide twenty-seven as opposed to the twenty-three concerts of section (a) and would make a stunning financial saving of 62.58%! If in this case the regional orchestras did twenty-seven rather than thirty concerts, the BBCSO might do a few more, and it could moreover be reserved for the very large works requiring many extras, a good many of whom might come from the Concert Orchestra. It could space out its programmes very comfortably. It it gave, say, fifteen concerts (three less than in the 1977 season) this would leave thirteen more concerts for chamber orchestras, miscellaneous contemporary music ensembles, and maybe a couple of visiting foreign orchestras. If the programmes were regularly proposed in full some seasons ahead, coherent design could result and the essential number of rehearsals could be scheduled in BBC time. New works could be given additional broadcasts before and after the Proms, as of course they sometimes are now — but there could be more of them, better played.

At the time of writing, cost figures for the 1980 season are not available (they cannot, it should be pointed out, be treated as secret by the Corporation; any licence holder is entitled in law to know what is being done with his money), and so a direct comparison with 1977 cannot be made. In 1980, moreover, the season was disrupted by the musicians' strike and some abnormal costs were incurred in cancellation fees. But it is quite realistic to estimate a relative expenditure in terms of inflated charges between the two years. If the 1977 concerts had been given in 1980, the cost would have increased by some 35-39% which, if we take the larger figure and apply it to the total of (b) (cost of using BBC regional orchestras consistently), would give £82,864.85, which is still £58,162.74 short of the 1977 total of (a)! The relation between (a) and (b) would have been similar, with adjustments for different scales (rail fares increased by a little under 41%, and the BBC's rate of subsistence payments by something less than 34%. Each year costs will inflate, but the basic argument is not likely to be undermined. Even if the total of (b) is doubled, it is still less than that of (a) by 15.45%!

Whether the Proms make a profit or a loss (a variable factor), the savings could be immense and the command of repertoire incalculably improved. Too often the Proms contain contributions from what has been dubbed the Rentaconcert system — something some-one else has already done elsewhere, at the Festival Hall perhaps, repeatable with minimum rehearsal cost. Often such items are worth having and sometimes the prospect of a Prom repeat has encouraged their origination. The performance standard is frequently high. But it cannot always compensate for lack of freedom in planning, and the money saved could be well spent on studio concerts with non-BBC orchestras, producers devising interesting programmes. Financial worries may also bring disturbing risks; that the BBC now permits the mention of sponsors on the air could be interpreted as the thin end of a dangerous wedge. In that case how much freedom will the planner get, and how far will the programmes have to be aimed at full houses? We are already familiar with the sponsors who have made little impression on the unadventurous repetitiousness of 'safe' concerts, night after night, at the Festival Hall in London. What will happen to the BBC's independance? Commerical sponsors, after all, want big audiences to read their names in the programmes. The BBC could pre-empt such threats by using properly the great and under-rated resources it already has, and nothing could have been more stupid or short-sighted than the attempt to get rid of a whole symphony orchestra for unconvincing financial reasons.

This raises the question of standards. Furtwängler once remarked that there were no bad orchestras, only bad conductors — a short answer to some-one's silly question. There is some truth in it, though radio studio conditions are not the best to encourage high artistry from conductor or players, and one cannot be certain of judging the full potentialities of either. The common impression that radio orchestras are workaday teams that will give a merely efficient account of whatever is put in front of them cannot be confirmed when these orchestras are heard under optimum conditions — especially in public concerts, which are essential to their well-being. There they are most stimulated, but the quality of their best studio work should not be forgotten. With the right conductor it may hardly matter whether there is an audience or not, for it is the conductor who can create an atmosphere in which the musicians are making music to each other. It is erroneous to suppose these orchestras incapable of extremely fine playing; the innocent ear will often refute this notion. All the BBC orchestras are in fact made up of self-respecting musicians of high competence, who will respond only too readily to proper direction and treatment; the standards by which they are auditioned are exacting, and not only in the matter of sight-reading (for which they are nevertheless justly celebrated). If they become bored, that is not always their fault, and avoidable circumstances sometimes prevent them from being on their mettle. At their best their achievements should be surprising only to opinionists. This has been so for a long time.

Many years ago in the early 1950s I played a recording of the *scherzo* of the *Eroica* Symphony to some senior BBC colleagues and asked them to guess the orchestra. They all suggested Berlin, Vienna and other such possibilities; it was in fact the BBC Scottish under that difficult but sometimes inspired man, Ian Whyte, and it was a studio, not a public, performance. In those days, moreover, there was no tape editing and everything was recorded direct on discs; no retakes were possible. Two or three years ago I picked up a performance (just missing the first few bars) of Nielsen's alarmingly difficult Sixth Symphony, a work I happen to know rather better than any of my own; it was one of the best I had heard, technically and musically, concentratedly sensitive and alive. I wish to apologise to all concerned for the fact that I was surprised to find it was the BBC Welsh under Janos Fürst, and the orchestra has since confirmed the impression in the same work under Norman Del Mar. In the 1979 Proms there was an outstandingly vivid performance of Shostakovich's Tenth Symphony by the Scottish under the brilliant young Simon Rattle, who more recently got from the same ensemble remarkable results in Mahler's *Das Klagende Lied*. Almost at the time of writing there has been a distinguished and powerful *Symphonie Fantastique* from the Northern conducted by Edward Downes, again encountered with an innocent ear after it had begun, and this orchestra has reached a consistently very high standard in recent years; its playing (on a tour in Germany) of the Ritual Dances from Tippett's *A Midsummer Marriage* under Raymond Leppard could scarcely have been surpassed. It has also recently played Tippett's First Symphony with a considerable *élan* under Bryden Thomson and given a revelatory performance of Mahler's Ninth under Kurt Sanderling. All this music is of marked difficulty and scope. The standard attained was in each case worthy of any occasion. More frequently than they might care to admit, the most reputable orchestras have been known to give mediocre performances, at Prom concerts and elsewhere. There is the strongest possible case for showing the boldest confidence in the BBC orchestras.

If each of these, under conductors of high calibre, were asked to be responsible for something like a quarter of the Prom season, the challenge would evoke a trenchant response, the more so if each orchestra's visit were limited to three nights, to minimise fatigue. Everything would be thoroughly prepared, in weeks rather than days; there would be a friendly rivalry, much interest in this from the Prommers, and a repertoire of range and cogency at present beyond reach. Give them superb conductors and they will play superbly, and the best conductors are not necessarily those most difficult to engage; the resident conductors should be appointed with the Proms specifically in mind, and offered appropriate salaries, efforts being made to find native talent before bringing in foreigners. The need for extended preparation of programmes would mean that the resident conductors would do most of the Prom concerts, guests taking part as and when practicable or desirable. With the best available soloists the results would elevate the powers and reputations of these under-valued orchestras and bring immense credit to the BBC. Those who imagined there was anything to gain by disbanding any of them would be very properly confounded, and the Scottish Symphony Orchestra should be restored to its correct size without delay. The opportunity of at once raising the standards of BBC perfor-

mance, widening and concentrating the scope of the programmes, and saving a lot of money should, if reason
prevails, shatter the mere politics that seem so far to have
ruled the reflexes of those on whose decisions these matters
hang.

It has been observed that programme-making is often
made difficult by the intransigence of conductors. It is true
that some will usually try to avoid learning things not likely
to be useful on the circuit, but it is also true that expecta-
tions of this can cause a planner to take the line of least
resistance. Every BBC producer knows this problem. But
most conductors are happy to appear at the Proms, and if
these appearances are seen to depend on a readiness to expand their repertoires, the changes of heart will be many.
No-one is indispensible, and talent is often discovered *faute
de mieux*, most likely for less money. At all events, the
scheme of the Proms must be above personal reputations
and whims; given proper time in advance, it will always be
possible to find the right performers for it. The planning
could have no better aim than Henry Wood's: to propagate
a conscious desire for the music itself rather than for the star
performer. Glock's extension of the repetoire was an advance, but there is still a long way to go. Control of
resources and therefore of repertoire is the key. If the programmes themselves are exciting and their *enchaînement*
lures the ear and mind from one to another, if they are finely
played, no one will complain. Wood's avowed educative in-
tent might be carried even so far as to enable the Prommers
to discover that the silence after the last note is part of the
music.

4.REPERTOIRE

IN THE post-war days of the Third Programme, it was impressed on a new producer that the content of the programme came first, then the choice of performer. It is a sound rule, still much applied. The order of priority could not always be preserved — visiting celebrities would have to be engaged with whatever was currently under the fingers or in the voice, or artists themselves would suggest interesting ideas, in which case the quality of the idea would decide acceptance, especially when there might be a choice between musicians of comparable accomplishment (one of the least enjoyable aspects of being a BBC producer is the necessity to sit in regrettably subjective judgement on one's fellows). At any time, of course, there may be a performer of such fascination that the choice of repertoire becomes almost irrelevant. Selection is inevitably a difficult and often complex business, and there were and still are checks and balances to prevent, if possible, over- or under-use of artists; without satisfying everyone, these applied throughout normal broadcasting but seemed to have a no more than marginal effect on the Prom programmes. The Proms, moreover, have in the last twenty years relied rather more on artists' repertoires than they ought; the use of non-BBC orchestras and their own conductors must tend to restrict the choice of music unless large sums of money are spent on extra rehearsals, assuming these conductors and orchestras to be free for them. Soloists will tend also to impose their touring repertoires. If it had been the established BBC tradition to perform the Proms largely with its own forces, the suggestion that more outside bodies should be engaged would certainly have been rejected as both extravagant and restricting.

There have been two revolutions in the Proms, one

gradual, the other more abrupt. To attract an audience in the 1890s Wood was obliged to offer the customary dog's dinner of the time — cornet or concertina solos, light ballads, popular salon pieces — interspersed with more serious matter. It was not long before the serious material was taking up half a concert (which was as long as a whole concert nowadays), and he set the practice of having certain nights for certain composers. It would be hard to conceive a better way, in the circumstances, of creating a new public for such music, served in increasingly concentrated doses as the audience got used to it. The audience itself changed, no doubt; some must have faded away as the programmes became more substantial, but they must have been more than replaced by music-lovers who needed serious concerts at low cost. By going regularly on Fridays you could familiarise yourself with almost all of Beethoven's orchestral works, or on Wednesdays with Brahms's. You could gorge yourself with 'bleeding chunks' of Wagner every Monday, and there were nights for Bach, Handel, Haydn, Mozart. Every night after the interval there was lighter fare, but even this was slyly modified, and you might find yourself faced with a serious first performance to start the second half.

Two practical factors made it possible for Wood to expedite this. First, the brutal simplicity of one rehearsal per gigantic concert (does the sight-reading genius of British orchestras originate in this?), together with Wood's rigid adherence to a timetable and his totally reliable beat. Second, a hand-picked orchestra to do all the concerts (Strauss said it was one of the best in Europe — he must have heard it without too many deputies). Despite lack of rehearsal and the insidious deputy system, and *pace* much dissatisfaction with the level of performance, Wood's technique made everything surprisingly safe most of the time. The deputy system enabled the players to send substitutes to the rehearsals or concert if they found more lucrative engagements elsewhere; a foreign conductor visiting London is said to have expressed his gratitude to one player at the end of the final rehearsals:

> 'I have noticed that you are the only member of the orchestra to
> have been at all the rehearsals — I really must compliment you.'
> 'Thank you, sir, but unfortunately I can't come to the concert.'

Later, when this system had been got rid of, and still more when the BBC Symphony Orchestra took over, the Prom standards could rise to considerable heights. They were at last wholly serious concerts and countless young listeners, including this one, learned the repertoire at Wood's feet.

The second revolution came when William Glock transformed everything almost at a stroke. Wood's pattern, which the committee had been continuing in its sleep, was expunged, the music came from a much wider choice of period and medium, one-composer concerts became rare, and there was a far more adventurous concentration of contemporary music, though at the expense of large areas, as we have seen. Familiar classics still found frequent places, but dispersed and without regularity. Glock argued with some energy that the 'central' repertoire was by now continually available at other concerts (of which there were many more than there used to be) as well as on radio or records. This 'freed' the Proms to become a festival of wider reach, stretching not only its repertoire but also its legs — some concerts were at places other than the Albert Hall, sometimes on the same evening, timed so that you could just about scramble from one to the other. This practice has not yet been abandoned.

The whole spirit and atmosphere of the Proms were completely altered; Glock had no doubt snatched them from a fate worse than death. It is not the aim of these pages to criticise *per se* his vigorous imagination, or, for that matter, the programmes of his successor. We are concerned with our principle, and with future possibilities. But it should nevertheless be said that in the enlivening of the programme some obvious artistic dangers were not escaped. Freedom tended to diffusion, perhaps reflected in the variety of venues as well as items. The desire to move with current trends led to the unjustifiable exclusion of much valuable twentieth-century music that was either not fashionable or failed to meet with Glock's approval. Individual concerts were frequently striking, but there was never a season with strong cohesion; the stress was as much on surprise as on meaning. Sometimes there seemed to be a touch of desperation — string quartets (and, in 1981, a piano trio) in the Albert Hall! There was still plenty of great music, but its centrality was in danger — too often it seemed a reminder of the best as foil to ear-tickling or tail-chasing.

Since in any period most contemporary music is worth very little, no one can avoid in our time continually encountering Last Week's Composer; perhaps he achieved rather too much eminence in these seasons. It was a move on the side of generosity, and Glock's constant search for the new did bring to light much that we would not have missed; but the area searched was too narrow for too long, and there was much we did miss in fourteen years that might have enriched our experience. These are personal impressions, essentially out of place here; others have different views. But the time-factor involved is ineluctable and our principle insists. It is not silenced by the present basically similar but less strikingly purposeful approach, and it whispers in our ear that it is now time for Revolution No. 3.

William Glock's flair and intelligence make one wonder what the Proms would have been like if it had occured to him to make full use of the BBC's forces; it is indeed intriguing to imagine the management's reaction (or perhaps lack of it) if Glock had unilaterally imposed the entire scheme recommended in this book — he would very likely have got away with it, and even with making his own appointment of a series of planners if he so wished. But our conjectures must concern the future. Let us examine Glock's contention that the central repertoire of great music is widely available elsewhere. There are in fact only two great composers *all* of whose major orchestral works are regularly performed at ordinary public concerts — Beethoven and Brahms. All the others are represented by a small handful of works each. Only four or five of Mozart's piano concertos, for example, are heard at all frequently in public, and not many more of Haydn's symphonies. Whichever indisputably great master you think of, you will find many of his masterpieces rarely played at the Festival Hall or anywhere else where audiences go. A lot of this marvellous music is more often broadcast, and much of it is to be had on records, but that is surely no reason to deprive the young Prom audience (many of them unable to afford big record collections) of the chance to hear it regularly performed in live concerts. There is still no substitute for a living performance in the living presence of people, and there is a great central gap to be methodically filled. Properly organised, the BBC's resources could do it. Henry Wood systematically propagated what became the best-known classics; what is left over is a much larger body of equally important music.

That is one big, basic thing that could be done, which has nowhere been done in public; it could form a broad ground for general planning and leave plenty of room for manoeuvre and plenty of space for further essential matter — new works, other contemporary music, pure entertainment, as well as the more popular masterworks of all periods. Using staff orchestras consistently would make calculated discovery possible — cycles of symphonies or other genres rarely heard complete in public concerts; composers highly regarded in their own countries but not much known here; schools or trends, old and new; composers the planner feels are unduly neglected; particular kinds of choral works; the growth of a certain kind of music; various sorts of orchestral virtuosity; sequences of works prompted by the same or similar poetry or philosophy — there could be several streams in any one series of fifty-odd concerts, and this is not the place to make detailed recommendations. The opportunities are endless, provided they make magnificent concerts and not didactic demonstrations.

Impracticable? No — once the planner has drawn up his scheme for a season (having been given what information he needs about the sizes and availability of the orchestras and the possibilities of augmentation) it can be thoroughly vetted by the Concerts Manager, who can then, with the help of the producers, explore the suitability and availability of conductors and soloists and get some idea of the costs. All this must be done two or more years ahead. The heads of the regional music departments will be much involved in the choice of artists, especially conductors, to work with their orchestras. If the booking of an artist has to be more than two years in advance, it is very likely that it will concern the same planner (supposing he does a stint of five years); if not, the next one may or may not be interested. The programmes come first — then find the performers! Programmes and objectives may have to be modified as arrangements proceed, but this is normal, and would be much less disturbing than at present, when decisions often have to be made too quickly. The prime constituents are the orchestras themselves; once their schedules are planned with the conductors and soloists, the rest consists of adjustments. The BBC, with its unsurpassed knowledge in the field, would be responsible for casting the programmes.

To reject all this on supposed practical grounds makes no sense. Henry Wood may very well have been told that no-one could possibly conduct fifty enormous concerts on successive nights (Sundays off) with one rehearsal per concert, the orchestra sight-reading itself silly, and the audience totally stupefied. If something is worth doing and the spirit is there, and the work is correctly prepared, a sound administrative routine will soon present itself. The BBC has all the necessary machinery at this moment. Some-one should wind it up.

5. THE PLANNER

IT HAS been suggested with some plausibility that it would be difficult, even impossible, to find suitable planners to take over from each other at prescribed intervals. In any country with an active musical life this should not be an insuperable problem, still less if the catchment area is enlarged. An organisation which produced the Third Programme during the post-war time of economic dearth ought not to blench at a difficulty of this kind. It seemes to me much more difficult to find the right man to do the work for fifteen years than to choose three, or five, to share it by instalments, each productively influenced, positively or negatively, by his predecessor. My first idea was that the planners should not be BBC personnel, but the music staff in 1981 includes more than one person of sufficient distinction and imaginative vitality; there is no reason why they should not be asked, and their immediate accessibility would be no disadvantage. By 1985, 1990, 1995, 2000 — who knows? Optimism is more creative than timidity. In the choice the musical profession should be consulted; there are a number of bodies whose views could be sought — The Incorporated Society of Musicians, The Composers' Guild of Great Britain, The Association of Professional Composers, the BBC's own music production staff and its own Central Music Advisory Committee (a lay body), the various contemporary music organisations in Britain and abroad, and a number of other professional concentrations of different kinds, all involving people of standing. It is unrealistic to imagine that a few inspirations would not emerge, and two or three would be enough for a considerable time.

If the mandatory period were three years, four planners would take care of twelve years; if four years, sixteen seasons; if five, twenty. It is far more difficult and hazardous to try to find the paragon, the miraculously unprejudiced saint and scholar, the prodigy of objectivity, the imaginative genius, the administrative virtuoso to do it, unsullied by even the slightest accumulation of injustices, for the rest of his working life. It would be decidedly presumptuous to assert the existence of such a person or the possibility of the BBC management finding him. The best of us is enough beset by personal bias to damage severely anything over which we have power unrestricted in time, no matter how intelligent, wary, or inclined to objectivity. Hope lies in getting the best sequence of people that can be found.

It is clear that the planner must be a person of wide and deep practical knowledge of music; administrative experience could be useful, but not essential, since the mechanics can be dealt with by the proper staff. Knowledge creatively used by a lively and passionate imagination must enable the planner to conceive a wide-ranging but coherent season; persons with the necessary qualities are often creative in other respects — it may be a composer, a performer or a scholar who will be found most likely to develop fruitful thoughts. It is less probable that the professional administrator or the impresario will have the solid musical knowledge and understanding to produce genuinely illuminating ideas. A practical musician, moreover, should know what musicians can do with a given amount of rehearsal, or how much stamina may be needed for a programme — it is to be hoped that no one again asks the BBC Symphony Orchestra to play *Le Sacre du Printemps* and Bruckner's Seventh Symphony in one programme; the brass section is unlikely to forget this concert. (It was not a Prom, as it happens).

The choice of planner need not be confined to Britain; it must be remembered that, with the BBC's forces properly exploited, he or she need do little more work once the season has been mapped out. To do this would take far less personal time than being embroiled in its administration (as the present Controller might well agree) and if the planner were not at once accessible at a moment of crisis needing a musical decision, there would be competent people on the spot to deal with it, keeping as closely as possible to the spirit of the scheme. This would be part of the agreed and contracted arrangement, and the BBC would have the right to make necessary though apt programme or casting alterations if the planner were not available. Such changes would be small relative to the whole — no more than now occur regularly. The Controller, Music could revert to his original function as arbiter, honest broker, host, administrative decision-maker for Music Division. He would have no personal, authoritative choice of the Prom planner or, for that matter, of BBC permanent conductors (these, too, should in my view be selected after much open discussion in Music Division); such authority would be inappropriate in a person appointed only by a decree of the Board of Governors on the advice of the management.

It must be asked why it is that BBC management posts (usually of Controller and upwards) are so rarely advertised, why the management therefore gives the impression of a self-perpetuating *élite* (a term some of its members are inclined to use against many intelligent people; it is strictly more germane to a self-elected group than to a number of individuals with similar cultural values). There have so far been only three Controllers, Music. The first, as we have seen, was installed by simple transfer sideways within the Corporation; this is a perfectly normal procedure, and it could be sensibly argued that the new post needed a seasoned BBC adminstrator to preside over the re-organisation. For the other two vacancies, however, there were no advertisements and no transfers from inside, no clear opportunity for the most capable, gifted, or experienced candidates, in or out of the BBC, to apply. On this level this seems to be general BBC practice. No-one, inside or outside, gets an inkling of what is afoot. Rumour is rife; one nightmare is conjured after another, sometimes in jest, sometimes in earnest. There is eventually an abrupt announcement and the new incumbent thuds into the seat.

Neither the management nor the Board of Governors can claim knowledge of all the best possibilities, or the right to rule out fair consideration of all comers. If a mistake is made, it is a big one, and the manner of its making is all too likely to bring about a closing of ranks in its defence or denial. Human history is rich in examples of the phenomenon. In the BBC its origins must lie in Reith's practice of personally choosing immediately subordinate companions in the first days of the organisation. If there was a vacancy at this level Reith usually invited someone to fill it. An inspired choice of this kind was Adrian Boult, but normally the *élite* seems subsequently to have refreshed itself to its own satisfaction, though not always to every else's. A structure of this sort is liable to produce a moribund inbred regime in any big concern, and to antagonise the professional element. One must ask how far the BBC management is self-selecting and self-preserving, and how frequently the Board of Governors rejects its recommendations in the matter; if the question itself suggests unfounded suspicion, that is because justice is not seen to be done.

From this type of background comes the good old British cult of the amateur. As often in large outfits, the staff member above a certain grade (say, in broadcasting, a producer) is periodically invited to an interview with one of the top brass — 'Are you happy in your work? Is there anything we could do to improve things in your department? Any questions you'd like to ask? Any suggestions you want to make?' There might be a tasty excerpt from the employee's Personal File (hidden behind the interviewer's forearm); it may be complimentary, or not, and comment is invited; or the conversation might drift into amorphous mists.

Imagine such an encounter. The interviewee has the temerity to enquire why a specialised channel is presided over by a layman rather than by expert staff under an expert chief, who could do it all with greater know-how and dispatch. 'Oh no, no — we mustn't let the experts loose — disastrous! The specialists would all ride their hobby-horses and the programme would soon be totally indigestible' (the mixed metaphors convey a characteristic atmosphere). 'You've got to have a watchdog for the sake of The Man in the Street' (If only The Man in the Street would stay there!) The trouble with the watchdog theory is that the postman calls much more often than the burglar.

We must ask, and clearly, whether a Controller, Music, if selected *in camera* by a seemingly self-chosen executive which has no specialist musical knowledge, and which gives him the job for a time limited only by his age, is likely to be a better choice as ruling spirit for the Proms (or for Music Division) than some-one entrusted with the task for a prescribed period and appointed by the BBC after thorough consultation with its own music staff and the profession at large. The management may very well protest that wide advice is taken in making such momentous decisions, that the Board of Governors has to be consulted and is ultimately responsible. But what is the exact competence in this field of the Board of Governors? If there are safeguards, why are they not seen to be applied? Nor is there any explanation of why the Controller, Music post has never been advertised. It is common knowledge that it is not normally possible to obtain a producer's job without answering an advertisement and attending a representative board, sometimes augmented by some-one from outside, either to give expert advice or to see fair play. Why is this not seen to be the rule with managerial appointments? The Association of Broadcasting Staff, for the sake of its members, should pursue relentlessly these disturbing questions.

6. IN THE OPEN

IN APRIL 1978 Radio 3 broadcast a tribute to Sir William Glock on his seventieth birthday. With the somewhat whimsical explanation that a programme of nothing but compliments was to be avoided, I was asked to take part, presumably because it was well known that William's views and mine diverged radically. Great respect for his musicianship had not prevented me from thinking him wrong about important things, and the hope that the respect was reciprocated was not diminished by the absence of illusion about his opinions of mine. Not wishing to seem an even slightly dissenting voice on a happy occasion, and certainly not wanting to spin pure compliments that would to some sound insincere when they were not, I at first declined. But after some thought it occurred to me that here was a chance to make the point about the Proms without any kind of personal attack; if they wanted a touch of the devil's advocate, why not? A simple principle could be aired on a BBC programme and the BBC itself would be the publisher. So I agreed to do it, a brief contribution expressing genuine admiration for William's musicianship, imagination, courage, for his constant quest for something new, this last activity indeed sometimes stifling us all with so much fresh air as to induce claustrophobia! — followed by the suggestion that despite what he had achieved at the Proms, the dangers of one man's exclusive control for fourteen years had become all too evident. I quoted the lists of composers to be found on pp.8 & 9 with a reminder that performers were bound to be equally affected, and made it clear that this criticism would hold good no matter who had done the job for so long. Unfortunately the producer's editing reduced it all to the barest bones, and it consequently sounded more like a brusque sally than was intended. But there was no malice in it, and none seems to have been imagined.

The subject was now in the open. Patric Standford, Chairman of the Composers' Guild of Great Britain, knew of my intention and raised the question with his committee. The CGGB then contacted the Solo Performers' Section of the Incorporated Society of Musicians, of which the Warden was John McCabe. Jointly they sent the following letter of 19 June to Sir Michael (now Lord) Swann, Chairman of the BBC Board of Governors:

Dear Sir Michael,

The Composers' Guild of Great Britain and the Solo Performers' Section of the Incorporated Society of Musicians have in recent years become increasingly disturbed at the planning and organisation of the Promenade Concerts. From 1960 onwards the Proms have been under the direct control of one person, i.e., the BBC's Controller of Music, and while one can only applaud the many excellent things that have been done under this arrangement there are large areas of music, in terms of both repertoire and artists, which have been seriously (and in some cases, totally) neglected during this period.

There are considerable dangers in having an indefinitely prolonged monopoly, no matter how open the person may be to ideas from outside. It is inevitable that any director of such a series of concerts, constituting as it does a major contribution to our musical life, should have a determined personal vision of the sort of programmes he or she wants to produce. But it is equally inevitable that his personal vision should incorporate strong prejudices in favour of one composer or artist against another.

From 1960 to 1973 the Proms were under the undoubtedly visionary control of Sir William Glock, and they are now in the hands of Robert Ponsonby who has followed much the same lines of choice. Without the slightest disrespect to either of these personalities, we feel it a matter of great importance to our national musical life for this system of organisation to be changed. We would be strongly against a return to the pre-Glock system of running the Proms by committee — on the contrary, we feel that they must be organised by one person in the way that Glock initiated — but we feel equally strongly that the period of control by each person should be restricted to three, four, or five years (five would seem to be an ideal time) so that every so often fresh impetus is given to the planning of these concerts, and a new mind, with new ideas about the image of the Proms, should run the show. It is essential that the appointment should not be renewable, so that change and a fresh point of view would be evident with each new appointment. Only in this way, we feel, can a truly fair balance of repertoire and performers be reached over a long period of time.

Yours faithfully,   JOHN McCABE
                                                                        PATRIC STANDFORD

Since I had given Standford notice of the intended broadcast and found his views similar to mine, it would have been less than human not to hope for some such response. But it was up to the CGGB to decide what, if anything, to do; I was not then a member and could have no influence on what must have been a committee decision. It could not be assumed that any committee would agree either with me or internally, let alone take any action. Many professional musicians for obvious reasons are loath to tangle with the BBC. Nor could I be in any way involved in the drafting of any letter if, indeed, any such thing were to emerge. It was thus the more satisfactory that so clear an awareness was shown of the need to stick firmly to the question of principle, not to let red herrings spoil the scent, to eschew irrelevant criticism of the programme-building or the individual views of this or that Controller, and to avoid the slightest whiff of personal attack, or suggestion of pressure on behalf of narrower interests (numbers of British composers or performers, for instance). The dangers of being misunderstood in such a matter are severe, and events proved it so. Journalists were continually having to be told that this was *not* an attack on Robert Ponsonby.

It should surprise no one that the McCabe-Standford letter is so close to the views already expressed here; we were all in agreement about the principle itself, which is simple -

and clear; faithfully rendered, it leaves little room for ambiguity. Ambiguities, however, may be found in plenty
elsewhere, and it was there that Sir Michael's elaborate reply sought to direct his correspondents' attention.

The Chairman began by agreeing that it was a matter of
importance and by expressing surprise that it had not been
brought up at meetings of the BBC's Central Advisory
Music Committee or at the BBC's standing committee for
discussions with the Composers' Guild, so questioning the
urgency and force claimed for it. This point has been dealt
with above; delay in putting a view does not in any case in-
validate it, and the Chairman's agreement that it was a matter of importance somewhat weakened his point. Sir
Michael next asked whether a change every three to five
years was really necessary or desirable. Not referring to the
question of principle, he went on to plead that William
Glock ran the Proms for fourteen years without any loss of
verve and originality, and that surely his choice of programmes was more catholic than the letter seemed to imply,
remarking that his successor, too, ranged widely round the
repertoire. We may reasonably suggest that this alleviated
no misgivings about the risks of long-term monopoly, and
that nothing was added to it by his next comment, that
given that the Prom season was a very short one (!) it
covered a tremendous amount of ground. Fifty-five concerts
that did not do that would be indeed remarkable. The Chairman then observed that there was no discernible *public* de-
mand (his emphasis) for a 'new mind, with new ideas about
the image of the Proms'. Any experienced public servant
must be aware that the arousal of public feeling requires
either high and costly organisation or provocation of
somewhat spectacular kind; that the BBC has not received
letters or telephone calls is not evidence.

The BBC Chairman followed these apparent prevarica-
tions by saying he felt the letter exaggerated the degree to
which Robert Ponsonby operated independently; that Ponsonby himself was on record as saying that he took advice

41

from respected colleagues. Surely it was unnecessary for Sir Michael then to insist that he believed this; in any case no-one had expressed any doubts of it, and it made no difference to the formal position in which the dangers reside. Napoleon was open to suggestion. Sir Michael Swann then did not spare his correspondents the notion that if the Proms were to be organised by a different person every few years, that person would surely have to be the BBC's Controller of Music (*sic* [1]) for that period, the justification being that the Proms were such a major event in the musical life of the nation that the BBC, which sponsored them, could not have a Controller of Music (*sic*) who was responsible for output that he was powerless to control. And as his responsibilities went far beyond the Proms, the consequences of the CGGB/ISM suggestion would be to impose upon the BBC the necessity for frequent changes in an important post, the duties of which range far more widely than the matters which caused those changes. The BBC could not accept that position.

To all that there is a clear response — the job-description of the post of Controller, Music is not immutable, as Glock himself comprehensively demonstrated. If the terms of the post were aptly defined according to the proposed new system, Controller No.3 could do the work originally designated, that is, the job done by Controller No.1 before it was unilaterally enhanced by Controller No.2. One may well ask: if the Controller, Music is responsible for the music output of the BBC, how much influence does he have on, say, television music?

The next point in the reply was described as purely materialistic. Could the Proms be made to pay? Sir Michael said that at the moment the BBC found it difficult to break even on a Proms season, but that this was not an excuse for playing safe and confining the programmes to those great composers of the past who were still the ones most likely to fill a large concert hall. The current statistics (1978) were proof of that. There were only (!) 55 concerts in this short (!)

[1] The correct title is 'Controller, Music'. Neither the Chairman nor the Managing Director, Radio got it right in public correspondence.

season but 14 of the 80 composers represented were living British ones. That seemed to him a very satisfactory proportion and about as high as the BBC could safely go. To compare it with the relative conservatism of earlier years (despite all the devoted missionary work of Henry Wood and others), was to realise how great an advance had been made since then. He believed that the BBC had made an enormous contribution to that advance by educating the public taste to a better appreciation of contemporary music.

Who had suggested otherwise? We may further observe that relative to the contemporary climate, Wood's Proms (certainly for a period longer than 14 years) were quite as adventurous as Glock's. The Chairman went on to say that people may differ about which living British composers should be featured, but the fact was that more than 200 British ones had had their works played on Radio 3 in 1977 and, as shown above, they comprised more than one-sixth of all the composers whose works were to be heard at this year's Proms. The BBC must retain in its own hands the power to regulate the speed of this advance: its policy, first enunciated by Reith as long ago as 1924, was 'music for all', and the person who had the final say in the Prom programmes had to accept that policy and that responsibility. The BBC could not give anyone *carte blanche* to indulge his own preferences to an extent that would change 'the image of the Proms'.

Carte blanche is exactly what the BBC allowed William Glock to take.

The CGGB and the ISM were not complaining of the quantity of British music played on the radio or even at the Proms. They were simply trying to put across a straightforward principle, which was in no sense recognised in the reply. There is not a single scrap of evidence in this or in any other BBC letter on the subject, to individuals, societies or the press, that the basic matter at issue has been given a moment's thought.

Imitation is the sincerest form of flattery, though mimicry

is unlikely to create the same effect. This thought was prompted by a letter I came across in *The Guardian* on 31 July 1978.

It was Swann's letter to McCabe and Standford, word-for-word bar a few trivial cuts and editings, signed not by him but by the Managing Director, Radio, Aubrey Singer, whose memory the Musicians' Union will always hold but may never cherish. It was used as a reply to a restatement of our principle by Patric Standford in response to an article (15 July) misinterpreting the case as an attack on Robert Ponsonby. The two BBC gentlemen Swann and Singer being on the same side, the one's apparent mimicry of the other cannot be construed as unfriendly, and the true authorship of this work presents a diverting problem. But there may be a drastic cause for the rather clumsily contrived duplication: the financial straits of the BBC are part of the national malaise, and economies are imperative. In 1978 nobody seems to have had the inspiring thought of announcing the demise of five orchestras; making one letter do for two staff was perhaps a hopeful start.

The correspondence drifted on, by post and in the press, and eventually petered out in a maze of false trails laid by some well-meaning letter-writers as well as less ingenuously by the BBC. The postal exchange ended from the BBC's side with a letter fom Swann (19 December) to both the CGGB and the ISM Solo Performers' Section (the ISM as a whole had not been embroiled). He noted that the subject had been discussed at the Composers' Guild [2] and then indicated that, at the request of the Board of Governors, discussed very fully at the October meeting of the BBC's Central Music Advisory Committee, where opinion amongst the widely varied membership was strongly and unanimously in support of the way in which the Proms were at present being run. He pointed out that that view emerged after a debate which ranged across a wide area and at which the specific CGGB/ISM criticisms and others were fully considered.

[2] Surprising! But this must have meant the BBC 'Composers' Guild Standing Committee'.

The Chairman further wrote that within the BBC itself opinion had been equally unanimous in supporting the present policy[3]. His Board had congratulated Mr. Ponsonby on the success of the 1978 season, and he himself knew that Ponsonby's senior colleagues, headed by Aubrey Singer, Managing Director, Radio, were warmly in favour of the work he was doing. They believed as did he, that Ponsonby conducted this complicated and rather thankless task with great skill and effect, and with a keen appreciation both of the work of living composers and performers[4] and the views of his professional staff. He added that the Proms continued to receive the enthusiastic support and appreciation both of the concert-going public and of radio and television audiences. He ended by saying that of course it was right of his correspondents to pass on the views of their members and that he was glad they had done so. He thought they should know that the result of a careful examination had been a resounding verdict in favour of the present policy.

Regrettably the committee of the ISM group accepted this euphonious farrago but Patric Standford and the CGGB stuck to the point:

'unfortunately we cannot find anything in your letter to answer our fundamental complaint that it is morally indefensible in a public corporation to allow one person, whoever that may be, to dominate Promenade Concert planning over an indefinite period of time'.[5]

Since then (October 1980) the CGGB with its new chairman Derek Bourgeois has revived the subject. The feeling was that a willingness to compromise should be shown, and Bourgeois telephoned Robert Ponsonby to ask if it would be possible for a representative of the CGGB (and perhaps also the ISM) to attend any Prom programme discussions that might be held, not in order to influence decisions, but hopeful of reporting satisfaction with the fairness of the programming

[3] Was the Music Division staff asked, or was the unanimity limited? I know the answer but may not disclose it.

[4] What was going to be done for dead performers?

[5] Letter dated 26 January 1979.

one to observe on behalf of composers, the other for performers. Ponsonby said he had no power to invite outside observers to such meetings, but suggested that Bourgeois write to Gerald McDonald, chairman of the Central Music Advisory Committee. He did so, and the reply was swift and in the negative, the idea dismissed as not worth putting on the CMAC agenda, with some thoroughly sound remarks to the effect that the Prom programmes could not in any case be planned by a committee, that an individual mind was needed. Excellent — but what does it really mean? If it is in any way authoritative, does it suggest there is no group discussion? How systematically and on what scale does the Controller take advice from respected colleagues? Does it reach proportions significant enough to threaten his imaginative vision or artistic bias?

Envisage a by no means preposterous situation in which producers, worried about a possible decline in the vitality of the Proms, persuade an incumbent Controller to hold regular concentrated meetings with them in order to try to expand the imaginative range. If the Controller does not soon feel that his identity is being invaded, and put up a resistance, it will not be long before the committee is merely chewing its way through much gum of dubious consistency and anxiously struggling to discover a synthetic identity; the ensuing decline into amorphism will be worse than that originally feared. The sheer scale of the Proms will eventually defeat any committee that does not, like the pre-Glock one, have a comfortable pattern to fill each season — with consequences we have seen. If the Controller finally defends his views in the only way left to him, by pulling rank, it could prejudice good will. One who resists the idea from the outset may be a man of character, but he evokes our principle in naked form.

Without inferring reality in this conjectural situation, we may note that in the 1981 Prom prospectus Robert Ponsonby repeated his own reaction to the pressure already put upon the BBC:

THE PROMS and Natural Justice

It is sometimes suggested that the Proms represent the prejudices of a single editorial mind. This is not, and could not be, so: no one person could have an expert knowledge of the vast range of music now eligible for inclusion. A sensible editor will rely on his advisors and contributors. That has happened this year, as usual, and I am grateful to many colleagues, part cularly to Peter Dodd, Misha Donat, Hugh Keyte, Stephen Plaistow and William Robson for help with the programmes.

The acknowledgments to colleagues appear to indicate a democratic policy but the personal power remains undiminished. No Prom planner can do without specialist advice, any more than could Napoleon, and no reasonable man is likely to ignore valuable suggestions. The planner nevertheless has the authority to act alone, and his periodic replacement can be the only certain safeguard.

7. MEMORANDUM

IT IS remarkable that since the days when Wood's pattern for the Proms was applied almost by rule of thumb the BBC, with its great resources, should have been unable to find a way to devise this festival with the kinds of consistency and purpose that are as possible as they are desirable. You can of course have one without the other, or the two things may not be of kinds to marry. Lack of purpose was no suitable reproach for Glock, nor even lack of a certain consistency in the way his predispositions tended to colour rather than construct the Proms. The whole somehow created an impression of the haphazard when compared with the old system; there seemed to be insufficient compensation for the patent want of large-scale planning. Individual concerts often encapsulated this tendency. There was something strongly attractive in all this, but the mosaic accumulation of each season became itself something worryingly inevitable, a negative norm. Like a kaleidoscope it threw up unexpected delights, and its animation was greatly preferable both to the old scheme and to any grim consistency suggesting didacticism. Nevertheless it should be possible, as I have already proposed, to infuse consistent purpose without losing freshness — if you have the resources. If the necessary means are not available to you or if you omit to make the best use of what you have, *force majeure* will shape many of your ends. For a large orchestral festival of some fifty-odd concerts, one almost every night of the week for eight weeks, you will need an orchestra a night and a lot of money. For a while the BBC seemed to be trying to demonstrate that it could mount the whole thing with its own resources; it used the BBC Symphony Orchestra every night, and it is surprising that a fleet of ambulances was not required to take care of the consequences, and that the deputy system was not resurrected. The only person showing comparatively little distress was Old Timber himself. There is a legendary conversation between him and Sir Thomas Beecham:

TB: I don't know how you do it. It would kill me.
HJW: Yes.

But even in those days there was no need for this herculean endurance test. The BBC had the forces then, and it has still better forces now. The regional orchestras are now much superior to what they were, and their substantial contribution to the Proms is fully practicable (the matter of the orchestras' holidays, the Proms being in the summer, could be and would have to be sorted out, and rehearsal schemes would still have to accommodate their other public and studio commitments; there is flexibility in the system, as can be confirmed). The financial advantages of using them have already been shown and it would require impressive ingenuity to cast doubt on them. The money saved could be used to enrich normal studio broadcasting and to give the non-BBC orchestras some extra engagements, a boon to listeners and producers alike. In this way more music could be had for the same money. But also of the greatest value and, one hopes, attractiveness to the BBC, the prestige of the Corporation would be enhanced throughout the world; it would be regarded not only as the organisation sponsoring the great festival of the Proms — it would more than ever be seen as the preserver, proprietor, and developer of splendid musical resources and standards.

Objections to such measures are more likely to emanate from pessimism or cynicism than from realism, and would rightly be felt offensive by the musicians concerned if it were asserted that there might be a drop in standards, or that the Proms might suffer some loss of panache or box-office appeal. Loss of panache seems to some crucial, though I must confess to lack of sympathy with Sir Arthur Bliss's opinion that without panache music is nothing. Glitter is often in the ear of the beholder or only in the reputation of the supposed glitterer, and once it has become frequently clear that the BBC orchestras can shine as well as some better publicised bands there will be no problem. Fine conductors, first-rate soloists and plenty of rehearsal can take care of such things. As for box-office appeal, we must remember that this has a slightly different meaning if the costs are reduced by $62\frac{1}{2}$%! If they were cut by even 20% the situation would be much eased, but that is not the whole argument. Box-office appeal depends on reputations, and reputations are made, most likely, by performance. There might at first be some falling-off in receipts, but as soon as it became obvious that the standard was very high (and anyone not willing to risk the effort and expense of going to the Albert Hall could judge this on the radio) the audience would vote positively with its feet. It takes a little while to establish a new scheme, and the right kind of publicity can be effective.

Trusting the BBC orchestras to carry the Proms would result not only in an annual display of a corporate artistic asset. It would be bound to gather beneficial effects on the orchestras themselves. It is only in relatively recent times that the regional orchestras have undertaken foreign tours, and these have been successful, though perhaps they ought to be more representative of British music than is sometimes the case. Tours of this kind, if not too exhaustingly rushed, are stimulating to the players and can be good propaganda for British orchestral standards; but they cannot reach an audience comparable to that of the Proms, a world-wide audience that expects high achievement. An orchestra that begins as competent will be stung to brilliance by regular exposure at these concerts and by the artistic rivalry of its colleagues and peers in the same situation. Care can be taken not to over-tire the players, and a general rise in level of attainment will then prove itself in all their other less glamorous but equally important activities. It would ill become the BBC to deny this possibility, so betraying some want of confidence in its own auditioning standards, which are excellent. The orchestras consist of good musicians, a fact they steadily demonstrate even now, given the right conditions. But they have potentialities that have not yet been tapped. The results could be vivid.

But the greatest advantage of the proper deployment of the BBC's musical forces lies in the priceless gain in power over the repertoire, which would be crucially important even if there were no economies involved. An entire season could be conceived whole, with minimum anxiety about the feasibility of this or that, and even the unavoidable changes in details dictated by circumstances would not normally do serious harm to the total design. The Prom planner could be nearer to an architect than ever before. The architect designs the structure which the builders then erect, consulting him about details that may have to be modified. Nobody expects the architect to set about the bricklaying or welding, or even to oversee most of the work, for there are site-managers and foremen to do that; the architect may well want to visit the site at times, but he need not be omnipresent.

That is why the BBC's contention that only the Controller, Music can plan the Proms is so hapless a response, bred by the apparently supine acceptance of Glock's personal method as if it were some kind of law. As Patric Standford wrote to Sir Michael Swann (2 August 1978):

> Sir William was surely given 'carte blanche'; it is well known that he virtually took it for himself when he abolished the Prom-committee in 1960. Any new Controller will now inherit Sir William's new Prom-planning rôle, and it would seem that the BBC has now blessed the 'coup' and regards it as so much part of the Controller's job that if it were taken from him he would cease to be Controller! It seems incredible to assume that the introduction of a Prom-planner from outside the BBC on a short-term (three or four season) basis would necessarily mean changing the Controller.

Incredible indeed, and the planner from outside would certainly not have to be installed, or have to be a full-time employee (if that were the case the poor wretch would have to sign a contract that would remove his tongue). Would the Controller really not have enough to do, or not enough prestige, or authority over the broadcasting of music, if he did not plan the Proms? If that is so, it makes a good case for not replacing him at all when he retires, and for returning the music department to its old status. Very few musicians, or even, I suspect, members of staff would care two hoots about that so long as good music could be made and broadcast, and so long as whoever was in charge could gain and keep the esteem and goodwill of his colleagues. It is of the most vital importance that the person running BBC music should be a musician of distinction and have the deepest possible respect, both professional and personal, from musicians inside and outside the Corporation, whatever his official label for practical purposes. For these reasons he should not be anyone to whom power is or even appears to be of any personal consequence. Without imputing the problem to any of the three Controllers, it must be added that for these reasons the process of his selection must always be seen to be sound.

The choice of the Prom planner is an equally sensitive issue. It is worth stressing again that the problem of finding suitable persons, though critical, can too easily be exaggerated. If the decreed period were five years, four people could take care of twenty years, and during that time others would emerge as viable possibilities for the next twenty. Once the system were established the problem would more likely be one of choice than of search. There would be new interest at each change, with much speculation about the new planner's interests and the areas he might explore or neglect — and consequent periodic extra publicity for the Proms. Criticism would be freer and healthier, made in the knowledge that a change would come at the end of a known time. Why should a Prom planner have a longer run than a Prime Minister? Certainly the change at the end of a term would be much less painful than can be the successive repeals of each other's laws by alternating opponent governments. But the regularity of elections exists to uphold the very principle this small document is trying to maintain in one part of the world of music. The democratic process has its jolts, but in the long run the principle is essential to equitable behaviour, and applicable in all walks of life.

In a letter to *The Times* (10 October 1980) I outlined it briefly. This drew support from Hans Keller (we have always been spiritual allies and intellectual adversaries) and predictable opposition, not from the present BBC regime but from Aubrey Singer's retired predecessor as Managing Director, Radio — Howard Newby,who refused permission to reproduce his letter here. It can, of course, be consulted in *The Times* of 23 October 1980. If it had shown our principle invalid, it might have contributed fruitfully to the argument; on the contrary, all its contentions are disposable. The persistence of a practice, even with success, does not itself provide moral justification. The production of a list of neglected composers is not a mere game. Neglect at the Proms is not as a rule carefully balanced by inclusion in the BBC's normal music output, in which there are plenty of gaps that some judges consider serious. Keller's letter mentioned Benjamin Frankel, unrepresented at the Proms during the whole of Glock's regime; if Frankel is an important composer whose unjustified neglect the radio seems to have acknowledged, the Proms can scarcely be complimented on his exclusion for fourteen years. His chances would no doubt have been improved if there had been four or five planners instead of two in the last twenty years. Talent for devising a public festival does not in itself guarantee coherent and illuminating music-planning, and the Proms consist of nothing but music. There is, we may add, no automatic reason to suppose that the resident incumbent of the Controller's office, until he is put out to grass or goes to some remoter area, is the only possible owner of the requisite talent for making good concerts. The reiteration of matter irrelevant to the principle at issue creates no more than an impression that the BBC manage-ment, even in retirement, maintains closed ranks.

There were sentinels of the mind that could be stood down. [1]

So this thesis, revolving for better or worse around an ethical principle, can be summarised eightfold:

1. Very large financial savings can be made if the BBC deploys its own resources properly.
2. The funds saved will be usable for other music broad-casting; it would be logical to direct them to studio concerts for non-BBC orchestras.
3. Positive and effective marshalling of resources will result in nearly total command of repertoire for the Proms.
4. The responsibility placed on the BBC orchestras will produce a striking development in their standards of performance that will reflect much credit on the BBC itself.
5. The ability to plan and control repertoire well in ad-vance will make it completely practicable to change the planner from time to time.
6. A committee, to judge from past experience and tak-ing into account the scope of the artistic issues at stake, would be an unsatisfactory way of planning.
7. A conception of this kind must be distinctive and in-dividual, though based on a wide view of music.
8. The principle itself. It is not morally justifiable that one person should dominate the planning of this vast publicly funded festival, its repertoire and its casting, for an unspecified period; the purposes of equity may be served only by changing at suitable intervals the set of prejudices in charge.

The principle generated the thesis; the morality presented itself and it was necessary to find a practical way of serving

[1] P.H. Newby, *Mariner Dances*, Jonathan Cape, 1948

it. This seems to me the right way round, and I hope to have illustrated what should be the axiom (and if it is not the human race is finished!) that there must always be a practical alternative to what is wrong. If my alternative to this particular evil needs modification, the details should be amenable under scrutiny in action while preserving the principle. But this needs proof in trial; the track-record of the present BBC regime does not encourage the hope that it will be attempted. It would of course be possible to adopt the money-saving part of the scheme while cynically continuing to ignore the ethics that prompted it; a dense smokescreen of sophistry would have to accompany such a response. But so far the principle itself has not actually been rejected, though more negative than rejection has been the stifling silence with which all attempts to express it have been received. No — not silence — a barrage of irrelevancies has been the answer. Behind that, silence. Does it signify vacuity?Only disaffected malice would assert that, and there is none here. Some-one has suggested that in the foreign affairs of a country the pressures of internal decision-making tend to exceed their external causes in influencing what action, if any, is to be taken. Perhaps this shrewd theory applies also to the BBC.

There is still a way out. The principle has not been denied or disproved. Let the BBC either demolish it on solid moral grounds, or take its point. If they choose the latter they can now say, with truth and perhaps even some excitement, that new practicalities are worth trying. Indeed there will be no alternative for them, but the reward could well be the making of the Proms into a greater and more significant celebration than ever before.

8. AFTERTHOUGHT: THE COMPOSER AND THE AUDIENCE

THE PROMS have always fulfilled a clear responsibility to contemporary music, a duty the more pressing because they are run on public money and because their audience has a certain stability, both in the Albert Hall and on the radio. No single planner, engaged even for a restricted period, could be expected to know the full spectrum of new music at any given time throughout the world. In this field a committee could be valuable, even necessary, a research committee made up of BBC personnel, using fully the BBC's wide contacts at home and abroad. Much of this work is already done through the regular score-reading process entrusted by the music department to a panel of substantial musicians, augmented in cases of doubt by the staff themselves. Works are also brought to the Controller's attention by various interested parties. Knowledge of what is going on in most areas of modern music is therefore extensive and up-to-date (Richard Howgill once remarked: 'We must have the means to represent what we are afraid is happening'). Directing research with a special eye to the Proms would be a simple and useful further step, since the BBC's present intake of new music for consideration depends largely on what is submitted, what may be picked up from foreign radio tapes, or what may be found in contemporary music festivals. This certainly provides a wide range of information. But if the BBC were able to make firm and cogent programmes for a whole Prom season well in advance, it would become even more important to carry out a positive search for new matter, rather than to rely to a great degree on what presents itself. Provision must always be made, of course, for very new works, produced after the season has been essentially planned, felt to be striking enough to warrant early placing; this need not be a problem unless the music in question is for highly unusual resources — postponement in that case need neither surprise nor too severely disappoint the composer. The nature of commissioned works will normally be known in advance.

The Prom audience has already shown itself tolerant of nearly everything a contemporary composer can throw at it, and this demonstrates the range of material exposed at the Proms. It is right that the Proms should do what lamentably few public concerts will risk; most concert-promoters who depend on box-office takings will realistically avoid including present-day music that they know will halve the audience. Contemporary music tends to become segregated in heavily subsidised concerts, or in festivals devoted to it, and its audience becomes a coterie. This is an unhealthy climate for it, and the BBC itself is not guiltless of compounding the situation in studio programmes like *Music in Our Time*, which cannot avoid being a ghetto, unnecessarily so because there is no economic excuse for it. From time to time an established symphony orchestra will commission a new work by means of a grant from, say, the Arts Council of Great Britain; this it will perform at one of its regular concerts, usually for the first and last time. These performances are often under-rehearsed. They frequently illustrate the musicians' saying, 'The first performance is the last rehearsal', while at the same time showing off the astonishing speed with which British orchestral players can reach the point of being able to negotiate the most difficult scores. But there is no time for a considered artistic achievement, and many a new work has been dropped after its first 'performance' because although it has been placed in a concert it has not been heard at all. Being acutely aware of all this, the unfortunate composer sitting in the hall is the last to blame the orchestra for the fact that he is the only person in a couple of thousand (or maybe a few hundred thousand if the concert is broadcast) who knows that what is emerging is not what he had heard in his mind. In such conditions the critics cannot truly assess what they imagine they are supposed to be hearing. Only several performances, each more confident and free than the last, can put matters right. The BBC is in a unique position to see that this happens, and I would advocate an extension of the occasional practice that the Prom performance (or the Festival Hall performance by the BBC Symphony Orchestra) is not necessarily the first — it should be the first public appearance of the work, which will have already been given several times on the air.

In Britain the BBC sponsors the only large-scale public music-making that does not treat the box-office as a crucial consideration. The Corporation is concerned to recoup expenses and even to reap a profit if possible, and we have seen how it could move further in this direction if it made rational use of its own resources. The Proms do not have a captive audience, but it is one whose loyalty dies hard, and it has been proved possible to present it with fare that would empty the Festival Hall (as the BBC's own Wednesday concerts sometimes demonstrate!). So it is not necessary to exhort the Proms to adventurousness — only to say that when you can plan your adventures with real foresight they will become the more exciting and the audience the more discriminating. The Prommers have been called indiscriminate, and there is amongst them an element more demonstrative than discerning, an exhibitionist minority such as may be found in any large band of enthusiasts. But the whole audience, not counting the radio listeners, is considerably larger than that leaning on the rail in front of the orchestra. The opportunity to perform new music in public has been seized at the Proms as nowhere else, and a vital aspect of its presentation is the context in which it is heard. Only occasionally is there a 'fringe' Prom for a 'fringe' audience of the kind that will also frequent places where they display piles of bricks. The normal practice is to play new music in company with more familiar or traditional works, against which it must stand or fall, and this helps to bring it an audience as well as providing a perspective in which it can be perceived. The fact that this is noteworthy is disturbing, and raises the question of why contemporary music is often an audience deterrent, and why it is so often shovelled into a corner.

The composers themselves are not entirely blameless. One may fairly and sympathetically observe that audiences are apt to want to spend their money on what they know will give them satisfaction, but their unwillingness to face a new work is not always due to conservatism. Most music-lovers will grimace if the subject is broached, and the reaction reveals not caution but active hostility. Audience and composer have become alienated from each other, and it is only a small minority of concert-goers which experiences pleasurable curiosity at the thought of a first performance. The rest bases its response on what it regards as bitter experience, and this is not to be ascribed solely to a want of education in the matter. The bitterness of the experience is not altogether imaginary and it can evoke a proper reaction. Why?

The reasons are inevitably complex and diverse. In the nineteenth century the so-called romantics, in response to a changed human climate and reacting against what had become in inferior hands a moribund 'classicism', sought increasingly to reflect and glorify a growing illusion of individual freedom and the western world's fascination with 'progress'. The would-be rationalism of the previous century was being supplanted by technical rather than abstract thought; instinctively resisting this trend, artists became inclined more to the subjective and were faced with a contradiction amounting to a predicament. The personal was more closely and defensively cultivated and cherished. As the working people became perforce trapped and stereotyped in the industrial revolution, the artist was more consciously determined to be different from his fellows, and the cult of individuality became an obsession, often coloured by a forced sense of pathos or tragedy. This was evident in many different arts, but the Austro-German musical hegemony made certain that in music its weightiest manifestation was in Central Europe. Where a Beethoven had had to grow up to an *Eroica*, a young romantic composer felt obliged to make it his Opus One. The cult of personality was in a sense the cult of immaturity, and the fatal looseness of structure common in that time was due to the failure to achieve mature grasp of the means to artistic integrity. There were also new discoveries, in part extensions of existing roots, in part their breakdown. As the desire for personal projection became more widespread and extreme, the elements of breakdown became more influential, and it was from Central Europe that most of them emanated. New and priceless enlargements of human consciousness, some highly disturbing but inescapable, were made possible. But the higher the degree of subjectivity, the lower was the potential for artistic integrity, which demands the power of detachment. Schoenberg must have sensed this in instinctively seeking to salvage order from a growing welter, and other composers at the turn of the century found themselves looking for systems, or cultivating sets of personal fingerprints by which they could be identified.

All this time, the rate of change in society was accelerating, with confusing effect on the sensitive artist who had always needed time for thought. We may object by remarking that Mozart or Schubert could compose so fast as to preclude any apparent pause for thought; but theirs was still a time of relative social stability and absence of obvious material change, when the language of music was not being rapidly and radically transformed. The objection also leaves out of account the fact that, apart from Mendelssohn in its first half, the nineteenth century possessed no Mozarts or Schuberts, though it is tantalising to try to imagine what might have happened if Schubert had lived into the 1870's. Even in Schubert, the only composer worthy to have followed Beethoven, we can find evidence of new and not altogether bracing influences, and it may well be significant that Mendelssohn, as he moved in his short life further into the century, seemed to lose something of the felicitous genius and perfection of taste that at first made him comparable to the two earlier composers. The historical-philosophical-sociological approach to artistic matters is often hazardous; but discernible general trends have to be explained in broad terms. There is some excuse for the idea that the late romantic composer, bent on the colossal, extruded his vast and sometimes prolix masterpieces with protracted grunts and snorts; high aspirations could prove no more than ambitions, and if imagined inspiration brought quick results, they were apt to want substance. Mahler wrote his enormous Eighth Symphony in a very short time; its first part is solidly composed, but its second, from the first solo baritone entry, is thrown overboard into an ocean of shameless *kitsch* from which it is never rescued, least of all in the inflated ending, and it must regarded as one of his weakest compositions. Such dangers were always liable to trap even the most gifted and intelligent musicians; the higher they aimed, the greater the risk of bathos.

Self-consciousness to the point of fixation, an obsessive urge to project the personality in a rapid vortex of change — these conditions saw the breakdown of norms; the process proved too often self-defeating, and only a few spirits felt obliged to resist it. The result was not fruitful diversification, but a gradual growth in uniformity. When all are making the same effort to be different, only the sameness of the effort characterises the majority. Genius is still distinguished, but more by its dependance on sharply identifiable hallmarks than on the breadth of its humanity or the organic nature of its processes. Among the less notable composers of the twentieth century the sameness is not of the kind that gave the eighteenth a *lingua franca*; it is a monotony born of haplessness, of a forced conformism at length compelled to the meaningless in pursuit of the singular. The pace of

61

change in our world and the gigantic threat facing the species are dizzying to the artist; he may even declare himself the anti-artist, so contributing in his small way to the violence that is on the increase in society. Commercial pressures are such that the throwaway product becomes an object of contemplation and the artist, no longer the servant of patrons he can recognise, or conscious of a vitally receptive public, is victim to the pervasive mores methodically procured by the multinational corporations. Yet the public, ready enough to be hoodwinked by the advertisers of consumer goods, still retains a vestigial sense that music and the other arts ought to have more substance, more appealing humanity, some promise of permanence, a feeling constantly being confirmed by frequent encounters with the great masters. The average music-lover unsurprisingly suspects that something is badly wrong, though he cannot analyse it. He is intimidated into unreadiness to identify rubbish, and is not encouraged by a similar pusillanimity in the critics who, moreover, often disguise it by blinding him with pseudo-science. The result is an atmosphere in which for the first time in history it is possible to be thought a composer without being a musician. 'The Emperor's New Clothes' was never a more apt parable.

So composers cannot justly complain if the public regard them with plain suspicion; some are entitled to protest a little, but not against the public. Those who are sincerely and concentratedly striving to create mature work may fairly be angry at the trend that has bred an unreceptive and suspicious audience, mostly unwilling to risk the expense of concert tickets in these hard times. It is not surprising that promoters are equally unwilling to take their very much bigger risks, and it is a matter for relief and gratitude that something like the Proms exists to help restore the balance. The BBC's present immunity from entrepreneurial infections must be jealously guarded; the encroachment of commercial interests, however it may simulate altruism, must inevitably be a corrupting influence.

Another factor makes the composer's present situation different from any in the past. Imagine Haydn composing next week's symphony. He can see in his mind's eye every face in the audience that will hear it — there may be a few new ones, or some missing, but he is in the wonderful position of being able to say to himself: 'This is going to startle old So-and-so!', or, 'This'll kill 'em!', or 'Whatsisname's going to be moved by this — he always reacts to a beautiful modulation', or 'I won't be able to play for laughing when this hits 'em'!' This may have been a very real compensation for servitude, but the reality of human contact was more important; nothing could be more stimulating or rich in meaning than knowing, while you were writing it, who was going to be listening to your music in the very near future. Think of Bach slogging away at next Sunday's cantata; he might be wondering which of the choirboys he would have to clout next, but he would also be thinking, not of a collection of aristocrats such as Haydn composed for, but of the ordinary folk he would see in the church every week. These were people he would meet in the street or their houses; they were not an audience of social superiors, and he must have known many of them intimately, on an equal footing. To them he would have been able to say: 'Sorry about all those da capos, but if you had to knock off a cantata every week, you'd be glad to get away with writing only two-thirds of every aria!' The ladies who clutched tear-sodden handkerchiefs while Beethoven improvised earned from him a contempt the more vigorous because he knew them only too well.

What of the composer of today? It is indeed rare that he can compose for a known audience, and the one precious thing he can sometimes do is compose for known performers — a joy denied to electronic operators! Even if he writes chamber music, aware that the numbers listening will be small, he is unlikely to know them as an audience, which may or may not contain a few friends, who may or may not be visible in the Queen Elizabeth Hall or even the Wigmore

Hall. If his orchestral music is being played, he sits in a huge hall among thousands of others, and if he goes on the platform afterwards he sees only a vast sea of anonymous faces. A gladiator in the Colosseum could not have felt less cosy. If he is himself an *habitué* of the Proms he will surely know some of the grins in the front row of the arena, though he will probably be unable to identify them in his mind as he composes — assuming he is writing something specially for the Proms, which is not a regular occupation of most composers. Far more new works are done on the radio than in the concert hall. Here the audience is invisible, and not only that — it is incalculable and seemingly immaterial; the music seems to go out on the empty air. There may afterwards be a letter or two from friends or even strangers who heard it, and the realisation that his music can be heard at great distances is for the composer a weird stimulus that Haydn could not have begun to imagine. But the composing of it cannot be enlivened by thoughts of So-and-so or What-sisname. This is a most serious deprivation. One remedy I am at present trying is to get an articulate and intensely musical friend to describe the kind of symphony he would wish to hear, and then to try to oblige him. It is a little step towards Haydn's enviable condition, without the servitude.

INDEX